GO BLUE!

MICHIGAN'S GREATEST FOOTBALL STORIES

Steve Kornacki

TRIUMPH
BOOKS

Library of Congress Cataloging-in-Publication Data

Kornacki, Steve, 1956-
  Go blue! : Michigan's greatest football stories / Steve Kornacki.
     pages cm
  Includes bibliographical references and index.
  ISBN 978-1-60078-848-2 (pbk.)
  1. University of Michigan—Football—Anecdotes. 2. University of Michigan—Football—Interviews. 3. Michigan Wolverines (Football team)—Anecdotes. 4. Michigan Wolverines (Football team)—Interviews. I. Title.
  GV958.U52863K67 2013
  796.332'6377435—dc23
                    2013024458

This book is available in quantity at special discounts for your group or organization. For further information, contact:
  Triumph Books LLC
  814 North Franklin Street
  Chicago, Illinois 60610
  Phone: (312) 337-0747
  Fax: (312) 280-5470
  www.triumphbooks.com

Printed in U.S.A.

ISBN: 978-1-60078-848-2
Design by Meghan Grammer
Photos courtesy of AP Images unless otherwise indicated

My family has always been there for me, and so I dedicate this book to them. My wife, Mary, and my sons, Cheyne, Derek, and Brad, shared the experiences of covering Michigan football with me for so many years. And my parents, Steve and Ileen, and my sister, Dee, have always been so supportive.

I always got the biggest kick out of my father, after retiring from Great Lakes Steel, walking down to buy a Detroit Free Press, *and then taking pride in my stories with anybody in the store who would listen. Okay, he was bragging. You don't care for your parents doing that when you're younger, but at that point in time it warmed my heart.*

And I loved it when my family got a chance to experience covering the Wolverines with me. Like the time Brad and Derek got invited into Bo Schembechler's office for a funny conversation. And when Mary picked up the phone on Thanksgiving morning in 1991 and got a special thrill. The caller was actor Mark Harmon, who had read the letter I sent his mother, Elyse, asking to interview them in regard to Desmond Howard, who was about to become the first Michigan Heisman Trophy winner since their father and husband, Tom Harmon.

My wife also bought a Michigan "M" flag with a blue background and maize block letter to hang on the pole on the front porch of our home in Ann Arbor. I was mortified about that because I took pride in being an objective reporter. So I had her promise to just wave it in the family room during games. Years later, one of the boys spilled the beans. Once I was out the door and on my way to the game at Michigan Stadium, which was just a few blocks from our home, they would hang the flag on the pole.

Oh, well.

They've all always been big-time Wolverines fans, and we've enjoyed so many bowl trips and special moments together connected to the games. But they also put up with me writing stories and this book at all hours of the day and night and having to watch movies and TV shows while I banged the keys of a laptop computer. And they always loved my stories—even if I told some of them a few times too often.

And for that, I dedicate Go Blue! Michigan's Greatest Football Stories *to my family. Some of them even worked their way into a few chapters.*

CONTENTS

FOREWORD

I first met Steve Kornacki in 1976 when I was an assistant football coach at Eastern Michigan University and he was a young sportswriter at the *Eastern Echo* and the *Ann Arbor News*. Steve then covered the University of Michigan teams under Bo Schembechler, Gary Moeller, and me for the *Ann Arbor News* and *Detroit Free Press*. He was respected as a writer and as an individual. All these years later, I am delighted to write the foreword to this book of special memories and stories of the nation's all-time winningest college football program. If you are a football fan, you will truly enjoy reading this interesting and insightful book about these great teams, coaches, and players.

Every Michigan football player and coach learns, in one way or another and sooner or later, that he is part of something bigger than himself. In the weeks leading up to the 1995 season, I saw the tradition of Michigan football reveal itself in a powerful and significant way. In late June, a small group of former players and I were gathered in a Detroit-area restaurant to talk about the upcoming season. Dave Rentschler, a great Michigan Man who had played for Bennie Oosterbaan, suggested that I consider inviting former players to come to Ann Arbor to talk to the team about their experiences and what Michigan meant to them. He thought it would be great for the players, and I agreed. Every man I invited accepted, and what transpired was a number of wonderful conversations about the Michigan football tradition. They talked about their coaches: Fritz Crisler, Oosterbaan, Bump Elliott, Schembechler, and Gary Moeller. They talked about their teammates; they talked about the game and how it had changed; they talked about school and student life; they talked about leadership and perseverance and winning; and they talked about their love for Michigan and its traditions.

By the end of training camp, the 1995 team had displayed the passion, the toughness, and the work ethic to be a very good team. The players voted two outstanding leaders, Jarrett Irons and Joe Marinaro, as their captains, and we opened the season in Michigan Stadium against an excellent University of Virginia team. With slightly more than 12 minutes left in the game, the Cavaliers led 17-0. But an incredible, improbable, unforgettable Michigan comeback ensued. As time expired, Mercury Hayes caught a game-winning touchdown pass from Scott Dreisbach. 18–17 Michigan!

For many reasons, the 1995 team has a special place in my heart, and the Virginia game is among my favorite memories at Michigan. But when I think about that team and that game, I also think about all those legendary players who answered my call and returned to campus to encourage and inspire a younger generation of Wolverines: Chappuis, Zatkoff, Kramer, Barr, Maentz. Dierdorf, Kenn, Brandstatter, McKenzie, Mandich, Greer, Caldarazzo, Ron Johnson, Wangler, and others. *Tradition*! It is the magic of Michigan.

This love for Michigan has united Michigan teams down through the years. And when the last day of even the greatest career has ended and the last whistle has blown, each player and each coach possesses his own memories of the games, the meetings, the practices, the travel, and the competition. He remembers the good days and some of the bad. But memories have a way of fading. It is the relationships that endure and bring the greatest joy to most lives.

For me, there is seldom a day that I don't communicate with one of "my guys." Those coach/player relationships have evolved and are now friendships that have enriched my life in a wonderful way.

On the day before he passed away, Coach Schembechler addressed the 2006 Michigan Team. He told us,

"YOU ARE THE LUCKIEST GUYS IN THE WORLD!"

As always, Coach Schembechler was right.

Lloyd H. Carr
May 1, 2013
Ann Arbor, Michigan

INTRODUCTION

I covered the University of Michigan football team as my beat at the *Ann Arbor News* and then the *Detroit Free Press*, and I wrote features and columns on the Wolverines during each of the last five decades for those newspapers and other media agencies.

Bo Schembechler, Gary Moeller, and Lloyd Carr opened their doors to me, allowing for the behind-the-scenes perspectives in this book.

Every fan remembers Desmond Howard's Heisman pose after the Ohio State touchdown, but I will take you back to our trip to see David Letterman and Tom Brokaw the night before the trophy was presented in New York. And I will open the door to the coach's locker room at Ohio Stadium after Bo's thrilling last game in the Horseshoe for his stunning revelation; and we'll travel to the rebuilt house near Miami that was blown away by Hurricane Andrew months before Wolverines center Steve Everitt became a first-round draft pick by the Cleveland Browns.

It was my privilege to get a unique view into the magic of Michigan football. I know how special these glimpses and stories are to Wolverines fans because I started out as a fan rooting for this team.

My interest in Michigan began with the kindly little old man who owned a store next to the Wonder Well on Grosse Ile, which I rode to on my bike along with my best buddy, current Denver deejay Rick Lewis. The Wonder Well, which shot cold, clear sulfur water high into the air out of a pipe, had appeared in *Ripley's Believe It or Not!* Mr. Swan sold sodas, candy, chips, and fireworks in a cinder-block building next to it and befriended me and Rick. He told us stories about playing for Fielding H. Yost, the great Michigan coach, that captivated us. We doubted they were true but loved them anyway. Years later, I returned with my own sons to find a framed story on the wall and an even older Mr. Swan still there. The story detailed the life of the oldest living Wolverines football player, Don Swan, who lettered in 1921–24 on teams that went 25–3–2.

Notre Dame was my favorite team until two All-American running backs from my hometown, Trenton High's Eric Federico and Lance "Lanny" Scheffler, were signed by Michigan coach Bump Elliott. Rick's dad took us to watch them under the Friday night lights, and those players turned me onto the Wolverines even before they played for Bo and the team that upset No. 1 Ohio State in 1969.

This book moves on a trail that begins with Bo, continues down the paths of the program's two latest Heisman winners, Desmond Howard and Charles Woodson, revisits Ann Arbor days with Jim Harbaugh, Tyrone Wheatley, Denard Robinson, and Mark Messner, journeys along the roads and runways traveled with Carr on recruiting trips, and visits the purveyors of tradition renewed, Brady Hoke and Greg Mattison.

You will read the stories behind the stories of the 1997 national champions and find what makes and made the voices of Michigan football—Bob Ufer, Jim Brandstatter, Frank Beckmann, and Tom Hemingway—so special to their listeners. The stories should, to paraphrase Ufer, warm your "little Maize and Blue hearts."

My hope is that when you read the last page, you will want more. Enjoy!

Steve Kornacki
FOXSportsDetroit.com
April 1, 2013

CHAPTER 1

Beating Ohio State in 1969

What began as an upset snowballed into a dynasty. They had no idea what had been started that day in Ann Arbor. All the Wolverines knew at the time was that the goalposts were coming down, and they were going to the Rose Bowl.

No. 1 Ohio State—the defending national champions, 8–0 on the season, winner of 22 straight, bully of the first magnitude, and a 17-point favorite—was upset by Michigan 24–12 on November 22, 1969.

Michigan offensive tackle Dan Dierdorf would play in six Pro Bowls for the St. Louis Cardinals. Tight end Jim Mandich would play in four Super Bowls with the Miami Dolphins and Pittsburgh Steelers. They, like every other teammate interviewed for a 20th anniversary story I wrote for the *Detroit Free Press*, agreed that "The Game" was their highest plateau of achievement and emotion.

It remains one of the most famous upsets in college football history.

"If I could re-create any one day," Dierdorf said then, "it would be that one. It just didn't get any better than that."

Dierdorf rose through the broadcast ranks after concluding his playing career, doing the highly popular ABC-TV *Monday Night Football* games for 12 years beginning in 1987, and he now serves as an analyst of NFL games for CBS-TV.

1

Mandich, who died of cancer at the age of 62 in 2011, also found his niche in broadcasting and was the co-owner of a construction company. He broadcast Miami (Florida) football and basketball games and Dolphins games, had popular sports talk radio shows, and became a South Florida institution.

"It was very pure and real," Mandich said of that game in 1969. "I had a lot of emotional games in the pros, but what I always come back to in the meanderings of my mind is that game."

The victory became the cornerstone of something lasting. That was also the year of the Miracle Mets and Joe Willie's Jets. But where those surprise teams differed from the Wolverines was on the turn of the page.

The Mets and the Jets would again hit hard times. But the Wolverines were headed to four consecutive decades of excellence. Bo Schembechler, the first-year head coach, went on to win 13 Big Ten titles in 21 seasons. Gary Moeller and Lloyd Carr picked up the baton, and between all three coaches, the Wolverines claimed 19 conference crowns in a 36-year stretch beginning in 1969.

The greatest rivalry in sports was never more memorable or primal than in the decade when Bo took on his mentor, Ohio State's Woody Hayes, the reigning ogre of college football. The final score after their tug-of-war for Big Ten supremacy was 5–4–1 in Bo's favor. Either the Wolverines or Buckeyes won the Big Ten championship in those seasons. They shared it six times. The only other conference team to factor into it was Michigan State, which shared the 1978 title with Michigan in what would be Hayes' last season.

But what if the Wolverines had lost that game in 1969?

What if Hayes had again let the air out of their hopes?

"I think about that sometimes," said Don Moorhead, the quarterback who outplayed All-American Rex Kern that day. "It may have taken longer if Ohio State had won. It may have been years before Bo could've gotten kids excited about coming here. But after that, Bo was known to everyone."

Schembechler the anonymous is hard to recall. But before that game, he was simply the spunky student flailing at his respected teacher, hoping to land a punch. No. 12 Michigan was 7–2 and about ready to back into the Rose Bowl; a Big Ten rule barred Ohio State from making back-to-back visits.

"I was just a young whippersnapper then," said Schembechler, who was only 40 at the time of that game. "I was struggling with that team. But when we won, I knew it was big—real big."

His eyes lit up with the memory of his signature victory. He retired with 234 wins, ranking fifth in all-time victories among major college coaches, but he never had one victory that meant more. It was the seed from which a sequoia of a football program grew.

"What all of us on that team feel great about is being on Bo's first team and setting the tone for his program," said Glenn Doughty, who shared the tailback position with Billy Taylor.

Fullback Garvie Craw, who scored two touchdowns against Ohio State, worked for a government securities firm in Manhattan 20 years later. He died of cancer in 2007 at the age of 59.

"Bo says he was closer to that first group because he put us through a lot," Craw said on that anniversary. "We had to listen to all his B.S. But, you know, he was right. Everything he said was right. I still get goosebumps talking about him and that game."

Barry Pierson, the cornerback who intercepted three passes against Ohio State and returned a punt 60 yards, said, "Bo is an awfully good friend. I would do anything for him."

Pierson was the last player I contacted for the anniversary story. He had gone deer hunting in Michigan's Upper Peninsula near his home in St. Ignace. His mother checked his answering machine periodically and called me to say she would pass along the interview request when he called her. She noted that he would love talking to me about the game. And upon receiving the message from Mom, he left the deer camp to find a pay phone. It was freezing outside and inside the phone booth, but I sensed Pierson would have talked to me forever about this.

"The key to football is emotion," Pierson said. "Everyone played 150 percent for four quarters that day. Bo had us ready to do anything. I never experienced anything else like that day."

The adrenaline began flowing after the 51–6 victory at Iowa the week before. "I remember us chanting, 'We want Ohio State!' over and over again after that game," Jim Mandich said.

It continued that Monday when Bo read the scouting report and dared each player to be better than the Ohio State player at the same position.

The Wolverines scrimmaged that Tuesday for nearly two hours.

"Guys had to be dragged off the field after that one," said Dick Caldarazzo, a starting offensive guard who became an attorney in Chicago. "They worked us hard because they thought we were too high, too fast. But we said, 'Don't worry, we'll get higher.'"

The Buckeyes had beaten fourth-ranked Michigan 50–14 in 1968 with Hayes sending in his starters to score a two-point conversion at the end. The move was at the root of Michigan's motivation for the 1969 game.

"Bo didn't let us forget that," Caldarazzo said. "There were 50s everywhere, on our lockers, the jerseys, and helmets of the demo team. You couldn't get in the shower without passing a sheet with a 50.

"I can still see Woody Hayes sending in Jim Otis to score those last two points. I'll never forgive that S.O.B. for that, no matter how much Bo loved him."

Bo shoveled snow off the practice field with the freshmen that week. He detailed the tendencies of Kern and safety Jack Tatum, which would prove critical in the game. He did it all but saved the best for his pregame speech.

"Bo got up on a chair," said Doughty, who played eight seasons for the Baltimore Colts and was then the owner of an instructional video company in St. Louis. "He started like a symphony conductor, real smooth, then built to the high point. He said, 'Fellas, we've worked hard for this...' and the next thing you knew he was off.

"Bo said, 'How dare they say this is the Team of the Century? We're the Team of the Century!' Before he could finish, someone shouted, 'Let's go, Bo!' and the place went wild. Guys were throwing chairs and beating lockers down. It was like an earthquake, and we had to leave for our own safety. We were David going after Goliath, but not with a rock. We had a nuclear bomb. We were on a mission to kick ass. We were like piranhas, and Ohio State was the little fish. We could not wait to eat those little suckers alive. Psychologists would say we couldn't play on that emotion all day, but it lasted through the entire game and into the parties that night."

Kern ran 25 yards on the first play, and the Buckeyes got past the piranhas like sharks. They drove to the Michigan 10 on their first possession, but on fourth-and-1, Otis was stopped cold in the middle of the line. Middle guard Henry Hill was given the tackle, but safety Tom Curtis, who made two of his school-record 25 interceptions for the season in the game, said history should be corrected.

"I stuck him pretty good," said Curtis, who founded Curtis Publishing Co. in Miami after an NFL career that included winning a Super Bowl with the Colts. "Hill gets the credit, but I made the tackle."

Curtis was elected into the College Football Hall of Fame in 2005—six years prior to the Hall of Fame induction of his in-law, Lloyd Carr. Tammi, the daughter of Curtis and his wife, Debbie, is married to Jason Carr, a former Wolverines quarterback whose father coached the 1997 national championship team.

Michigan and Ohio State traded touchdowns twice before the Wolverines took a 24–12 lead at the half with 17 points in the second quarter. Nobody scored after the half.

The final touchdown run by Moorhead was set up by Pierson's 60-yard punt return. He stiff-armed and danced his way to the Ohio State 3-yard line.

"People still bring up that game all the time," said Pierson, who coached St. Ignace to the 1983 Class D state championship and later coached Whitmore Lake High near Ann Arbor. He also owned several businesses near the Mackinac Bridge. "I'm not sure why it was my best day. It was quite a one-day deal, but I wasn't a one-game man. I was completely exhausted when it was over and wanted to lie down on the field and rest. But I didn't come down off that high for three or four weeks."

The fans chanted, "Good-bye, Woody!" and Doughty said a celebration of Mardi Gras proportions carried on into the wee hours of the morning.

Woody met Bo walking off the field and said, "Congratulations." Bo was speechless. "I didn't say anything," he said. "I just shook his hand."

Things would never be the same.

CHAPTER 2

Bo Schembechler Tried to Fire Me

Bo Schembechler tried to get me fired.

There I was—28 years old and covering the Wolverines at the *Ann Arbor News*—and the legend himself called my boss and told him he wanted me canned.

Bo and I had our share of unsettling moments early on, and I began to feel a bit like those officials Bo chased up and down the sideline when they threw a flag he felt was undeserved. Back in my first two years on the Michigan beat, 1983 and 1984, I had no idea of what vibrancy, warmth, laughs, and triumphs I would experience with Bo in the years that followed.

How could I after that call he placed to *Ann Arbor News* editor Brian Malone?

When Malone retired in 2011 as publisher of *The Times* of Trenton, New Jersey, I called to congratulate him and wish him well on a life without deadlines. And guess what he brought up?

"You know," Malone said, "I'll never forget that phone call from Bo, wanting me to take you off the Michigan beat. He wanted me to get rid of you!"

Malone asked Bo why he wanted me removed, and he told my editor that I was ruining his recruiting efforts by publicizing their every move with the country's top players. Malone asked him if my reports were accurate, and Bo said they were. Bo noted a few other stories that I wrote that he didn't care for, and again Malone asked the same question. "Yes," Bo told him, "they were accurate."

"Steve will be covering your football team as long as I am the editor of the *Ann Arbor News*," Malone told Bo, who harrumphed and hung up the phone.

Had I been working for a spineless editor, I would have been covering Washtenaw Community College soccer or checking the want ads the next day. Bo was the supreme dictator of almost anything he chose to claim in Ann Arbor, so this was not as easy as an editor citing journalistic ethics and wishing some civic leader "good day" after stating his case. There were politics involved, for sure. But Malone stood by me.

Thirty years ago, there were no websites devoted entirely to the recruitment of high school athletes such as www.Rivals.com. For the most part, player commitments were reported when players announced them at their high schools. Many of the recruits received no publicity at all in the college town they selected until the school put out a list of those who signed national letters of intent on signing day each February.

But that approach was changing in the early 1980s, and Malone wanted me to aggressively report on who the Wolverines were pursuing, getting, and losing. Bo told me that he was at a recruit's house one night when I called. That irritated Bo because I interrupted his time with the player, and made him feel as if he was being followed. But the timing was purely coincidental.

Bo's anger with my "intrusions" reached a boiling point in regard to the recruitment of Andre Rison, the Flint Northwestern star who would go on to set Michigan State's career receiving yardage record that stood for nearly a quarter-century. He became an All-American and the first-round pick of the Indianapolis Colts before tearing up the NFL.

And Bo wanted him. Boy, did he want him.

But Bo wasn't going to get Rison away from Spartans coach George

Perles, and Bo had a theory as to one significant contributing factor.

"You *cost me* Andre Rison, damn it!" Bo shouted at me.

There was no, "Is this Kornacki?" There was no hello. Nothing. That's how the phone call began.

I took the call while sitting at my desk in the sports department and could not believe what I was hearing. Bo was talking and shouting so loudly, and he had such a recognizable voice, that a number of my colleagues were attracted to the conversation and gathered around my desk to eavesdrop.

Bo said my story, in which Ann Arbor Pioneer High receiver Cedric Gordon said he would commit to Michigan if he met academic requirements, had caused problems with Rison. Bo said Rison was upset because Bo had promised that he would not recruit another receiver in the state, and Bo then told me on the phone that there was no way he was going to sign Gordon.

I told Bo that after Gordon and his coach, Chuck Lori, confirmed for me that his intentions were Michigan if his grades and test scores were in line, I called him and Wolverines recruiting coordinator Fritz Seyferth to ask if Gordon was being recruited in light of his questionable academic situation. This can be a slippery slope for reporters and coaches because NCAA rules don't allow them to discuss recruits with the media. But I wanted to do my due diligence and provide both sides of the story.

Neither Bo nor Seyferth would comment about Gordon, either on or off the record.

"Bo," I said, "it has to be a two-way street between us if you want stories to include your point of view."

He shot back, "It's *not* going to be any damned two-way street. Got it?"

Bo liked to punctuate statements with "Got it?" when he was on a roll.

"Hey," Bo continued, "I've got to know one thing from you."

He paused for effect.

"I've got to know if you're for me or against me!"

I told Bo that I could be neither.

"I can't be your public relations man," I said. "And I won't be a hatchet man, looking to cut you down. All I can be is fair."

It was odd that Bo had no response to my explanation. Unless you can count muttering whatever he said under his breath as a response.

"Good-bye," he said before hanging up the phone.

I hung up my phone and turned to discover that I was encircled by my fellow reporters, jaws collectively dropped. None of them knew quite what to say, and so they just quietly walked away.

I sat there for a minute or two, trying to figure out what had just happened. What would the ramifications be with Bo and my pursuit of covering his team? Couldn't be good, right?

But that's where I was wrong. Something struck a chord with Bo after that strange conversation, and he began to warm up to having me around. Then he actually began to like having me on the beat. Bo started letting me into occasional practices, was critical in helping me break a few stories, and showed me another side that I never figured I would see.

I guess he just wanted to put me up against the wall and see how I would respond.

Everything was a test with Bo. He challenged everybody because he was that confident in who he was and what he demanded.

Bo once walked up to an oft-injured lineman sitting on the practice sideline with a bag of ice on his ankle. He looked the player in the eye and said, "How are you ever going to be anything here if you are always hurt?"

There was no time allowed for the player to respond. Bo quickly walked past him because he knew what the answer was. He always had things figured out.

"Got it?"

CHAPTER 3

Bo Schembechler Behind Closed Doors

There have been four Glenn Edward Schembechlers.

The one you know was born Glenn Edward Schembechler Jr., son of a Barberton, Ohio, fireman. Junior would not have been nearly as cool a nickname as the one his older sister, Marjorie, pinned on him when they were kids.

"My sister couldn't say 'brother' and it came out Bobo," he said. "Then one of the Bos was dropped. I was Bo ever since I can remember."

His father, known as Shem, wasn't much for sports. But he taught his only son to play by the rules at any cost.

"My dad left his job [at the Babcock and Wilcox Boilermaker Co.] during the Depression to become a fireman," Bo said. "He knew there was security there for him and us. Well, he works his way all the way up to captain and the fire chief retires. Him and another guy are going to take the test to see who gets the job. Barberton is a tough town, and it was corrupt. Well, the guys want my dad to get it so they want to hand him the test.

"They say, 'Look, Shem, we want you. So-and-so has gotten the test and there's no way the other guy can beat you.' My dad said, 'No way.' He wouldn't take it. He hung up the phone and was crying at the thought. He was so upset. Dad could've been it automatic, but he took it on his own and still only missed by a couple points. That had a hell of an impact on me. I made up my mind I was always going to be a straight guy."

Coach Bo Schembechler is carried off the field by Ed Muransky (left) and Bubba Paris after Michigan's 23-6 win over Washington in the Rose Bowl on January 1, 1981, in Pasadena, California. (AP Photo)

Bo paused. He shifted nervously in his office chair and leaned over the desk to add emphasis to the point he was about to make.

"But the one thing I was going to do differently was I was going to be a hell of a lot tougher. He was the man for the job, Dad was."

Shem's first two children were daughters, Virginia and Marjorie, and it wasn't until Bo assisted Woody Hayes at Ohio State that he took an interest in sports. "The guys at the Elks Club kept asking him questions," Bo said. "So, he figured he better get some answers." Bo had played as an offensive lineman in football and a baseball pitcher at Miami of Ohio, but his father just didn't have the love of sports that his son had.

"My dad died of a stroke in 1960 at the age of 60," Bo said. "He was up to Columbus the day before he died to see us play. My mom called the next morning and said he was lying on the couch watching television when he started gasping. He was gone in 30 seconds."

Bo was 40 when he had his heart attack on New Year's Eve, the day before the Rose Bowl game. He was walking up a dark road from the monastery where the team was staying in Pasadena when it occurred, and he was recovering and sleeping in a hospital bed while his team lost to Southern Cal. Bo asked a nurse for the score when he woke up.

He'd gained 25 pounds during his first year as the coach at Michigan and watched his Big Mac and Coke diet a bit better after that. And he began taking power naps on the gray leather couch in his office to get more rest, just like the doctor ordered. He had a catheterization before a quadruple heart bypass in 1976, and then he had another quadruple bypass after a 1987 heart attack.

I remember walking away from the locker room with Bo after a game at the Metrodome in Minneapolis and noting that he didn't look good at all.

"I've just been battling this cold," Bo said. "I'll be okay."

But another heart attack was on the way in the days ahead.

Finally, in 2006, his ticker just gave out in the final stages of terminal heart disease. His heart muscle would not respond to a pacemaker, and Bo was gone.

But he lived to an age 17 years longer than his father.

Shem never got to see his son become a national name in leading the Wolverines to even ground against Hayes and his big, bad Buckeyes. Bo had a 5–4–1 edge in the tense rivalry that came to be known as "The

Ten Years' War."

And Shem never got to see Bo's son, Glenn E. Schembechler III, better known as Shemy.

Shemy was Bo's only biological child. He adopted his wife Millie's three sons, Chip, Geoff, and Matt, after the couple married on August 3, 1968. The boys' biological father had died four years earlier.

And Shemy ended up being more like Bo's father—a gentler man. But Shemy did get Bo's love of sports and analyzing them. He was the football manager at Miami of Ohio, and he was a graduate assistant coach at Michigan in 1993. He served as a scout for the Chicago Bears for four years and then spent 12 seasons scouting for the Washington Redskins.

Shemy, the son of the greatest Wolverines coach of all time, was living in—of all places—suburban Columbus, Ohio, in 2012 when he visited the press box at halftime of the Michigan–Ohio State game. Instead of coaching for or against the Buckeyes, as his father did, Shemy scouted them along with other college teams.

The circle of life sure does take some crazy turns.

Shemy and wife, Megan, have a son, Glenn Edward Schembechler IV, and they decided to give him the nickname of Bo.

BO'S DISAPPEARING SHRIMP

We used to interview Bo in a basement banquet room at Weber's Inn in Ann Arbor after having lunch with him every Monday during the season. One Monday, after beating Ohio State, he was taking a particularly long time with the alumni he addressed before speaking with us.

The waitress put a shrimp salad on the table at his seat at the head table, and it sat there for maybe 30 minutes before Rich Shook, the veteran United Press International writer, decided to begin eating them one at a time every minute or so. Shook always sat to Bo's immediate right on those Mondays when we broke bread and talked football.

Shook ate all but one of the shrimp.

We couldn't believe he had the guts to pull this, but Shook knew what a cloud Bo would be floating on. Nothing could get him steamed after beating the Buckeyes.

Eventually, Bo arrived, all smiles. He greeted us, "Hello, men!" Then he sat down in his seat and surveyed the ravaged shrimp salad.

Silence.

Then a quick glance to his right and laughter.

"SHOOK!" Bo shouted. "Did you do this?"

"Yes, Coach," Shook said, "I cannot tell a lie."

Bo roared with laughter and cackled for joy. You could've flattened his car tires on the Monday after he beat Ohio State and he probably would've smiled and said, "I needed some new tires anyway."

And, oh, they brought Bo another shrimp salad.

Bo's Mom and His Highest Finish in the Polls

Bo Schembechler never won a national championship. He won 234 games in 27 seasons at Miami of Ohio and Michigan, but he did not finish on top even once.

What was his highest finish?

Oddly enough, it came with a team that neither went to the Rose Bowl nor won even a share of the Big Ten championship.

It was the 1985 team with the killer defense that finished No. 2 in the final Associated Press and United Press International polls. Those were the only two polls that mattered in the pre–Bowl Championship Series days.

And Michigan came to that finish in an odd, unlikely manner.

The Wolverines were No. 2 when facing No. 1 Iowa on October 19, 1985, and lost 12–10 in Iowa City on Hawkeyes placekicker Rob Houghtlin's chip-shot field goal at the end of the game.

However, despite a 3–3 tie at Illinois later that season, the Wolverines stayed high in the polls and capitalized on a domino effect of losses by other top teams. After beating Nebraska 27–23 in the Fiesta Bowl at Sun

Devil Stadium in Tempe, Arizona, the 10–1–1 Michigan team rose to No. 2 in the final polls.

I was staying at a hotel across the street from the Wolverines' team hotel in Scottsdale, Arizona, and decided to call Bo for a reaction. His 82-year-old mother, Betty, picked up the phone and said, "Bo isn't here right now. Boy, will he like this news! I'll have him call you when he gets back."

Bo called back, too. And he didn't even seem like he was grudgingly doing it because Mom made him. He usually shrugged his shoulders when asked about the polls because a) he could not control them and b) they were voted on by writers. But he was genuinely happy and thrilled about this finish below only the No. 1 Oklahoma Sooners coached by his friend, Barry Switzer.

"We'd like to be No. 1," Bo said, "but that will happen someday. I'm not in the poll business, but they're No. 1 in my heart. Still, it's a great accomplishment for us."

Michigan did finish No. 1, but it wasn't until 1997 when Lloyd Carr, whom Bo hired as a defensive backs coach in 1980, turned the trick. Bo's other top finishes were No. 3 in the 1974 AP poll and No. 3 again in both the AP and UPI polls in 1976.

But let's get back to Bo's mom. She was the only person on the planet who had any control over him until he married Millie the year before they came to Ann Arbor. And Bo got more than his fire from her. It was his mother who took him to Cleveland's Municipal Stadium to watch his beloved Indians and Bob Feller, and she fostered his love of sports. Her son also loved Notre Dame and Ohio State as a boy.

"I used to drag Mom out on Ladies Days and listen all the time on the radio," Bo said. "I read all the stories—all the box scores. Mom loved it."

I remember looking at the photo of Betty on Bo's desk and wondering how that kindly little old lady with gray hair and glasses could have lit such a spark under Bo. But looks can be deceiving, right?

"Mom is as tough as nails," Bo told me, referring to her as if she were Dan Dierdorf. "She's a good gal but a tough gal. Mom will set you straight. She's independent, smart."

Bo's father, Glenn Edward Schembechler Sr., died of a stroke when Bo was coaching on Woody Hayes' staff at Ohio State. It was Bo's mother who called him in Columbus with the sad news. She meant the world to him over the years, and Bo would stay at her house in Barberton, Ohio, with assistants whenever they were recruiting players in northeast Ohio.

The late Milan Vooletich, a defensive assistant coach, chuckled when telling me of a conversation he heard between mother and son as he walked down the stairs toward the two of them in the kitchen.

"You know how Bo is with everybody," Vooletich said. "He's gruff, doesn't take crap from anybody. I mean anybody. So there he was, talking to his mother in this real sweet, almost singing voice, 'Yes, Mommy...Oh, yes, Mommy...Of course, Mommy.' I couldn't believe it."

There you have it. The coach who peeled paint off walls and took his wooden yardstick to the ample behinds of 300-lb. linemen who could not space properly was putty in the hands of his mother—an unashamed momma's boy.

As much as I like to believe Bo called me that night in Scottsdale because we'd developed a good rapport, I knew better.

PEARL HARBOR REVISITED

Four writers sat around the breakfast table in Bo Schembechler's suite on the top floor of the Hilton Hawaiian Village in Honolulu, sipping coffee and discussing the win over Hawaii the day before and the Rose Bowl just more than three weeks away.

The view from Bo's 29th-floor suite was spectacular. The shores of Waikiki Beach, high-rise hotels and the mountains of the Waianae Range were glistening in the early morning sun on December 7, 1986.

Then the roaring whoosh of fighter planes broke the quiet paradise of the setting, much as Japanese Zeroes had on that Sunday 45 years ago.

"Look at those jets!" shouted Bo, pointing to the four flyers. They were crossing over Pearl Harbor at 7:55 AM, honoring the 2,403 men who died during the Japanese attack on that day of infamy in 1941.

The remains of the USS *Arizona* still rested in the waters off Ford Island in the distance. The sunken ship, which still drips oil to the surface, is a permanent tomb for many of the 1,177 who died aboard the battleship.

Bo spoke of his memories of World War II, which broke out when he was 12 years old. Sometimes you came for a football briefing and got a history lesson.

Bo's Final Game in the Big House

Witnessing the unbridled locker room euphoria of a huge victory is quite a show. The energy, love, and commitment of a championship team come together for a true passion play.

And I had no idea after Michigan's 1989 victory over Ohio State in Ann Arbor that the celebration was for the last of Bo's 234 coaching wins and 13 Big Ten championships. As we ran through the tunnel after the game, Wolverines equipment manager Jon Falk pulled me aside and told me to wait by a locker room door.

Everyone else in the media hurried to the news conference, but I waited there for Falk to open the door. And I got to be a fly on the wall as Bo stood on a stool in the center of the room and congratulated his players on winning the championship and Rose Bowl berth. He did so with fire in his eyes and a booming power in his voice. It was as if each word had an exclamation point after it.

Bo stressed that they had become men as surely as they had become a great team, and his players glowed with satisfaction. Coming from their tough-love coach, the praise meant even more.

Then he led them in a singing of "The Victors," all thrusting long-stemmed roses high in the air as they punctuated the song lyrics, "Hail! Hail to Michigan, the champions of the West!"

Any and all doubts were gone. The gassers run in the heat of two-a-day practices were worth it now. So were the sacrifices that went along with playing football at this level of competition. This was what they all came to Ann Arbor for, to once again realize the truth in the Schembechler mantra: "Those Who Stay Will Be Champions."

And what a Big House exit it was for Bo, the man whose teams began the streak of 100,000 attendance games that has gone on for so long, nearly four complete decades, that it's taken for granted.

But nothing was being taken for granted in that locker room. It was all about savored joy.

There are moments that you remember clearer and longer than the rest, and that scene has stayed with me as if it were yesterday.

BREAKING THE PENN STATE STORY

I was the only reporter who made it to the first Rose Bowl practice on a cold December night in 1989 in Ann Arbor. Nearly a foot of snow had fallen that day, but my house was just two miles from the indoor practice facility. I figured I could make it that far, and I ended up getting much more than a story about preparing for Southern Cal.

When Bo spotted me walking onto the sideline, he shouted my name and demanded I come to midfield. I knew something really bad or really great was about to happen. I jogged to meet him at midfield, where he stood holding the yardstick he used to whack linemen who weren't lined up correctly.

"Penn State is in!" he shouted.

I told him it was inevitable that Penn State was joining the Big Ten, but it was not official. Then he corrected me, saying that Big Ten officials had put the conference's athletic directors, including him, on a conference call that day with the news.

"Isn't it on the wires?" he asked. I assured him it was not, but he asked that I call my editor from the weight room. We didn't have cell phones yet. I called and spoke with my editor, Dave Robinson, and was told no such news had moved on either the Associated Press or United Press International wires.

Bo was fuming—not about the decision, but about the process. He said the athletic directors were never so much as "consulted" in adding Penn State as the conference's 11th member in a few short years.

"This confirms the worst fears I have of presidents getting too much control in athletics," Bo told me. "Making decisions like that without studying it is terrible. Not one athletic director was consulted on this matter. How can they do that?"

That quote went into the *Detroit Free Press* story that Jack Saylor co-wrote with me about the Penn State news.

What did not get into the paper was a confidential conversation with Bo that ensued.

"So," Bo asked, "do you think I should stay on as the athletic director after I coach this last game?"

He was still at near boiling point, and I knew he wanted me to say he shouldn't stay based on his body language alone. But I gave Bo the answer he didn't want: "Yes."

He barely let me finish before he bellowed, "*Well* then, you're dumb as hell! Do you think I should stay here and push pencils around on my desk all day long?"

Well, since he put it that way, "No."

And before long, Bo resigned as athletic director and took the relatively low-pressure job of being president of the Detroit Tigers for his good friend, Tigers owner Tom Monaghan—the same Domino's Pizza founder and owner who once gave Bo a Domino's franchise in Columbus for not taking the head coaching job at Texas A&M.

But there was another reason besides rejecting the pencil-pushing aspect of the job that caused Bo to leave Michigan. He didn't want to be so close that anyone would suspect he was looking over the shoulder of his hand-picked successor, Gary Moeller.

Bo knew how to make an exit.

Bo and My Boys

I was working out in a gym in Dunedin, Florida, on November 17, 2006, when the elevated flat-screen televisions above the racks of weights were constantly showing photos and clips of Bo Schembechler. I didn't think anything of it at first. Hey, No. 1 Ohio State was hosting No. 2 Michigan the next day, and it was a normal time to recall the glory days of Woody and Bo.

But after doing a couple different sets with the weights, I noticed Bo was still up there. Something was wrong, for sure. So I walked closer to the TV sets and read the caption: "Former Michigan football coach Bo Schembechler is dead at the age of 77."

My heart sunk, and I had to sit down on a bench to gather myself. Somehow, despite his heart surgeries and ailments, you always believed that Bo would live forever...that is the way it is with spirited, lively people. You can't picture them having time to die.

After recovering, I didn't know what to do. But a little voice told me that Bo would want me to finish this workout. So I did.

When I got to my home in nearby Palm Harbor, I opened the front door and saw my son, Derek, sitting in front of the TV in the family room. He looked at me with a pained expression. I could tell that he was trying to figure out how to break the news to me.

I forced a smile and looked at Derek, and said, "I know."

We watched the tributes and recalled all the stories, including our most special one.

I had a question for Bo one summer day in 1989. My sons, Derek and Brad, then 8 and 7, were with me running errands in Ann Arbor, and we stopped in at the football team offices. I left them outside Bo's office with his longtime secretary, Lynn Koch.

Bo noticed them as I walked through the door and waved them inside.

"C'mon in," he said, chuckling. "These your boys, eh?"

He reached across his big wooden desk to offer handshakes. Both of my sons looked slightly to the side, a bit nervous and shy about meeting the legend.

"I'm Coach Schembechler. And always remember that when you shake hands with a man, you look him in the eye and give him a good, firm handshake."

Years later, Derek told me the reason he did not give Bo the desired handshake was because he had chocolate from a candy bar gooing up his hand.

Bo had the boys touch the Rose Bowl trophy his Wolverines had won months before against Southern Cal, mentioned that he loved their crew cuts, and talked baseball with them.

Brad mentioned that one of their T-ball teammates "keeps throwing the ball to the enemy."

"The enemy?" Bo said. "You mean the other team?"

Brad nodded yes.

"I love these kids," Bo said. "Great haircuts, too. Wish every guy on my team had one.

"Keep hitting those liners," he added as we began walking out. "Come back again. Who knows? I may end up recruiting you guys. Wouldn't that be something?"

That memory made us smile on what had become a somber day.

My wife, Mary, called me from the local library where she worked. Mary didn't know if I had heard about Bo. We recalled the time they met in front of the team hotel in Honolulu and how sweet he was in talking to her. And then I lost it, just sobbed.

Tom Hemingway, the longtime Michigan football and basketball play-by-play announcer who lived not far from me along Florida's Gulf Coast, had discussed going down to Boca Grande some time that winter to have lunch with Bo. I'd run into Bob Thornbladh, who played and coached for Bo, that summer in Ann Arbor on a visit back home. He suggested I go see the "Old Man," as his players often referred to him, because he wasn't feeling good.

But Bo wouldn't be coming down to his Florida place after that season. He was gone, having lived a life that touched so many lives. And what more could be said of any of us?

BO'S WEDDED BLISS

You want to know who Bo's two best recruits were?

They were his wives, Millie and Cathy.

Without them, Bo would've been miserable. And miserable coaches are not successful coaches.

I didn't get to know Cathy other than in a few brief meetings. They were married in 1993 when he had already left the Detroit Tigers post that he held after leaving Michigan.

What I do remember about her was this silhouette in the distance of her and Bo at Folsom Field after a game in 1996 in Boulder, Colo. They were sitting on a bench near the press box elevator, and I didn't recognize who they were at first because of the late-afternoon shadows. But as I got close to the elevator, I could tell that the guy with his arm around his girl was Bo, and he was sharing the glow of a Wolverines victory with Cathy.

Bo was wearing leather shoes and no socks. I'm not sure why that made such an impression on me, but it did. I guess it was because I'd never seen him inside a stadium without wearing black coaching shoes and white athletic socks. And Bo just was not a guy who went around wearing pleated slacks, a sport coat, and no socks. Bo? No socks?

I chuckled about the socks and told him, "Bo, you must be loving retirement. You don't even wear socks anymore."

He was so happy that he laughed and agreed.

There were times when he could surprise you. I once asked him whose music he enjoyed.

"Tina Turner!" Bo said. "What energy, what a voice. And she can dance! What a gal."

He also went to a Neil Diamond concert at Cobo Arena in Detroit and met Elvis Presley backstage in Las Vegas after a show. But he wasn't all fun and no socks. There was the Bo who could be, well, a real old poop—especially at bowl games.

There was a dinner dance before the 1984 Sugar Bowl at the Hyatt Regency in New Orleans. Auburn coach Pat Dye was there with his wife, laughing and dancing close and gracefully. And there was Millie, Bo's wife, explaining how he was busy. Auburn, by the way, won the next day.

I once did a "Millie Schembechler Rose Bowl Diary" for the *Detroit Free Press* from the Newporter Hotel, where the team was staying in Newport Beach, California. His "boys" got Bo his second and final win in Pasadena to culminate that trip on January 2, 1989.

Millie explained that Southern Cal coach Larry Smith, who had been an assistant for Bo, and his wife, Cheryl, had attended a black-tie dinner at the Pasadena Hilton on that trip. Millie, of course, was not escorted by her husband.

"When we got back," Millie told me, "I told Bo he was very blatantly absent. He's never gone to it, and now everybody understands. I couldn't believe it the first year. Now I just tell everybody the truth—he's watching film."

She said Bo would have a second room on every bowl trip that was listed under an anonymous name. He would go there to watch film and be left alone. Film, for Bo and many other football coaches, is more addictive than anything that could be ingested.

The morning after they won the Rose Bowl, I went to the Schembechler suite, which was a condo with a view of rolling hills and a swimming pool. Millie was so gracious to find time for me during the week. And when we finished talking, she asked that I call my sons to their suite. She wanted them to see the Rose Bowl trophy and hold it.

Millie, who married Bo in 1968, didn't have much time left, though. When Bo retired one year later, he said he wanted to spend time with her. Then he became president of the Tigers, but that was a part-time job by comparison to being the coach and athletic director of Michigan. And there was no film to watch.

She died of a rare form of adrenal cancer on August 19, 1992, after an eight-month battle. Millie Schembechler was 63.

Their son, Shemy, who became an NFL scout, has stayed involved at the University of Michigan with the Millie Schembechler Adrenal Cancer Program and the Heart of a Champion fund named for his father that raises money to form treatments and promote therapies to fight cardiovascular disease.

CHAPTER 4

Ufer, Brandstatter, Beckmann, and Hemingway:
Voices in Blue

Michigan football fans have received the same passion and dedication from their longtime radio broadcasters as they've gotten from the coaches and players down on the field.

Has there ever been an announcer who wore his emotions on his sleeves more than Bob Ufer, who cried after calling Anthony Carter's 45-yard touchdown scamper on the final play against Indiana in 1979 and honked a Jeep horn for scoring plays?

Frank Beckmann succeeded Ufer after Ufer's death in 1981, and eventually formed an endearing team with Jim Brandstatter, a former Michigan lineman. They bring insider anecdotes, unabashed love of the Wolverines, astute observations, and true teamwork to the airwaves.

And if you wanted a baritone voice with a keen sense of storytelling, there was Tom Hemingway on the campus station, WUOM-FM, which fed a state-wide network. He was more controlled than the others, a sort of PBS voice of reason amid the exclamation points.

They are and were the Voices in Maize and Blue.

HONK IF U FER MEECHIGAN

Ufer was a Big Ten track star while attending Michigan during World War II, and he loved the school and its athletic teams with the fervor of a tent revival minister. You could hear the pain in his voice after defeats and

27

the glee in his words after victories. Objectivity is supposed to be observed on broadcasts, but Ufer was subjective from the first word of his play-by-play to the last.

And nobody rooting for the Wolverines complained. They laughed at his strange quirks—Ufer called their favorite coach "General Bo George Patton Schembechler" and their hated nemesis "Dr. Strange-Hayes"—and appreciated how he turned a big play into a bizarre trail of strange descriptions, adjectives, and adverbs.

The quintessential Ufer call came during the 1979 homecoming game against Indiana when Anthony Carter caught a pass from John Wangler at the 20-yard line, eluded a pair of defenders, broke a tackle at the 5-yard line, and pranced into the end zone with both arms held high and the football in one of them.

Ufer, his voice cracking with emotion and disbelief setting his tone, said, "I have never seen anything like this in all my 40 years of covering Michigan football.... Look at the crowd! You cannot believe it! You're listening to it. I hope you can hear me—because I've never been so happy in all my cotton-picking 59 years! I have seen—I have broadcast 347 ball games. I've never had one like this.... Meechigan wins, 27 to 21. They aren't even going to try the extra point. Who cares? Who gives a damn?"

And Ufer honked his General Patton combat Jeep horn through the merriment. Ufer once explained on a broadcast that Patton's nephew listened to his Wolverines football telecasts in Benton Harbor, Michigan, and sent Ufer the horn that had been left to the nephew in the legendary general's will. So, Ufer decided to honk three times for touchdowns, two times for field goals and safeties, and once for extra points. And if he really got excited, as he did on the Carter touchdown, Ufer would honk it as many times as he pleased.

He called Carter "the human torpedo" and proclaimed, "Bo Schembechler is looking up at Fielding H. Yost in football Valhalla" and thanking him after that dramatic, game-winning play. On his *Michigan Replay* show, Schembechler laughed, shook his head, and asked, "What is a Valhalla?" His co-host, Brandstatter, informed the coach, "It is the great beyond where all great coaches go to put up Xs and Os."

Neither explaining nor defining Ufer was easy.

Bo, in a quote posted at www.ufer.org, summed up Ufer. "He became an institution because he was different from anybody else...and the interesting thing about him is...he was genuine."

The "Meechigan" pronunciation Ufer used came from the way he heard Yost, the school's first great football coach, pronounce it in his West Virginia drawl. Yost, the cigar-chomping athletic director when Ufer met him as a track star, and future athletic directors Fritz Crisler and Don Canham were part of Ufer's classic description of Michigan Stadium:

"The hole that Yost dug, Crisler paid for, Canham carpeted, and Schembechler fills up every Saturday."

Ufer was 61 when he died of cancer during the 1981 season. He broadcast 362 consecutive games over 37 seasons, and yet he was an inspiration to his beloved Wolverines in the decades after his death.

Tom Brady, now the perennial Pro Bowl quarterback of the New England Patriots, is quoted on the Ufer website as saying, "Ufer's CDs are what Coach [Lloyd] Carr played to fire us up before the Ohio State game!"

Ufer's most memorable anti-Buckeyes rant came during a broadcast in 1973 when the Ohio State players tore down the M Club's "Go Blue!" banner being held up at midfield.

He spotted the co-captains of the No. 1 Buckeyes leading the charge onto the field and reported, "Here they come: [Greg] Hare, [Rick] Middleton, and the Buckeyes...and they're tearing down Michigan's coveted M Club banner! They will meet a dastardly fate here for that! There isn't a Michigan Man who wouldn't like to go out and scalp those Buckeyes right now. They had the audacity, the unmitigated gall, to tear down the coveted M that Michigan's going to run out from under! But the M-men will prevail because they're getting the banner back up again. And here they come! The Maize and Blue! Take it away, 105,000 fans!"

Ufer then allowed the roaring crowd to fill the next 30 seconds of his broadcast. That game ended in a 10–10 tie that resulted in a first-place tie for the bitter rivals, and the ending Ufer predicted did not come true. Wolverines placekicker Mike Lantry's 44-yard field goal with 28 seconds remaining went wide right.

The "Ufe" began at WPAG, a small radio station in Ann Arbor, and did his final seasons for WJR, which could be heard halfway across the country.

"Bob Ufer took me under his wing when I began doing games in 1963," said Tom Hemingway, who broadcast on WUOM for 31 seasons. "We became great friends, and when he was moving to WJR, he told me, 'You know, Tom, I called 'em and warned 'em. I told 'em that they were going to get calls saying that they have a crazy man calling their games.' Ufer was actually thinking of changing his style some, toning it down a bit. He was concerned. I said, 'Bob, don't even think about it. Be yourself.'"

He stayed true to his zany, "Maize and Blue" self to the very end. He would regularly attach the school colors as an adjective, and one of his favorites was, "Bless his little Maize-and-Blue heart."

When he did his last game on October 17, 1981, the Michigan marching band spelled out his name at halftime: "U-F-E-R."

The horn was done honking, along with descriptions like this one about Barry Pierson on a return against the Buckeyes in 1969: "Going down that mod sod like a penguin with a hot herring in his cumberbund."

Yes, Ufer really said that.

His style was unforgettable. That's why you can still find this bumper sticker in Ann Arbor from time to time: "Honk If U Fer Meechigan."

JIM BRANDSTATTER

Jim Brandstatter has been part of a Big Ten family feud that goes beyond his father and brother playing at Michigan State.

Most fans know that Brandstatter was passed over for a scholarship by Spartans coach Duffy Daugherty after his senior season at East Lansing High. But what you might not know is that his wife, longtime

Detroit television news anchor Robbie Timmons, graduated from Ohio State. So the voice of the Wolverines grew up a Spartans fan. And he married a Buckeye.

Go figure.

"Brandy was almost like a Jehovah's Witness for Michigan with all the people he had to convert in East Lansing and Columbus," his long-time broadcast partner Frank Beckmann said.

He had his work cut out for him but got the Maize and Blue converts.

"Robbie grew up in Columbus and went to Ohio State," Brandstatter said. "In 1971, when I was a senior at Michigan and Woody [Hayes] was tearing up the yard-markers, Robbie was in the stands in Ann

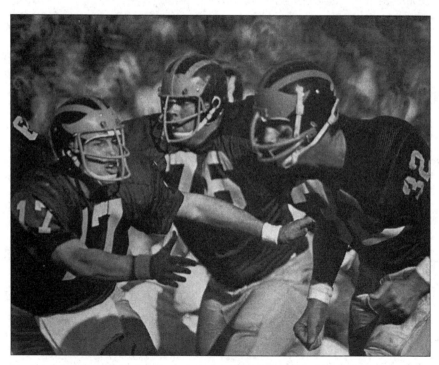

(Left to right): Tom Slade, Jim Brandstatter, and Fritz Seyferth during the 1972 Rose Bowl Game in Pasadena, California. (Image first appeared in the 1972 University of Michigan yearbook, *Michiganensian*, and is in the public domain as it was originally published before 1978 without a copyright notice.)

Arbor, shouting, 'Go Woody!' And there I was, playing on the field for Michigan."

One year later, they met while working at WILX-TV, then an NBC affiliate in Jackson, Michigan. They soon moved on to rival stations in Detroit and began dating. They were married in 1980.

Remember that ESPN commercial with the guy in the Ohio State T-shirt kissing the girl wearing the Michigan T-shirt? After they finished kissing, this message was super-imposed over the couple: "WITHOUT SPORTS, THIS WOULDN'T BE DISGUSTING." Well, switch the T-shirts, and that was Brandy and Robbie. But it worked.

Timmons is retired from TV, but her husband keeps going strong. Brandstatter has done the *Michigan Replay* and *Inside Michigan Football* shows with Bo Schembechler and the coaches who followed— Gary Moeller, Lloyd Carr, Rich Rodriguez, and Brady Hoke. And he has done the games on radio in four different decades.

The kid Duffy didn't want ended up accounting well for himself both as a player and then behind a microphone. Bump Elliott brought Brandstatter to arch-rival Michigan, and he played on two Rose Bowl teams for Bo before becoming a broadcasting institution in the state.

His father, Arthur F. Brandstatter, was an All-American fullback for the Spartans as a senior in 1936, and in 1961 he was named to *Sports Illustrated*'s Silver Anniversary All-American team. His brother, Arthur L. Brandstatter, lettered as an end at MSU in 1959–61.

"My dad was on the MSU faculty," Brandstatter said. "And boy, I was interested. My brother was my hero, and I was around the team a lot. But my brother had not had a great experience there, and my dad had some issues going on. And they did not recruit me. Michigan did, but even they were a late scholarship. It was Dayton, Navy, Central Michigan, and Western Michigan until Michigan came into the picture.

"And when I came down, I enjoyed Ann Arbor and the campus. And the guys on the team were neat guys. I wanted to play Big Ten football. I'm a Big Ten kid, and it challenged me. I played behind [All-American]

Dan Dierdorf but started my senior year. I told Dierdorf that I pushed him to greatness. He said, 'Yeah, you held my helmet during timeouts.'"

Brandstatter chuckled. That self-deprecating humor is something that he brings to broadcasts, too.

"But I played my two best games against our two biggest rivals my senior year," he added. "And I noticed the crowd in a different way. I remember throwing a good block on a screen pass that Billy Taylor scored on in Ann Arbor. I heard that roar of the crowd. And at that moment, I thought, *I can do this. I belong.* I did something good in a game when it mattered.

"It was a dream thing for me."

He worked as a sportscaster right out of college, and his evolution in the analyst role began with cable telecasts of Wolverines games before landing the *Michigan Replay* and radio gigs.

Brandstatter has been an analyst for every quarterback from John Wangler through Denard Robinson and now Devin Gardner. He has called the games of Heisman winners Desmond Howard and Charles Woodson. And he's marveled at great blockers such as two-time All-Americans John "Jumbo" Elliott, Greg Skrepenak, and Jake Long playing his old tackle position.

Did Brandstatter have a call that he treasured above all others?

"No," he said, "not really. I just get the biggest kick out of predicting a play at a key point in a game, and then having the team run exactly that play."

Brandy is an analyst's analyst. His love of the game's strategy and subtle nuances comes through loud and clear.

He also loves telling a good story on the air and has written a pair of books, *Tales from Michigan Stadium*, volumes one and two.

Some of the stories were short, like the huddle scene between Anthony Carter and Wangler on the 45-yard touchdown pass to beat Indiana: "Anthony looks at Wangler in the huddle, and just says, 'Don't worry. Just throw me the ball.' Now this is a freshman saying, 'Throw me the ball.' But Bo pretty much said the same thing on the sideline. It didn't matter if they were going to double-cover him."

Some of the stories were long, like the one he got from Wolverines All-American end Ron Kramer about spreading the ashes of his coach Bennie Oosterbaan, an All-American end 50 years before Kramer, around the Michigan athletic facilities in late October 1990.

"Ron and Bennie were close, and he visited him to the end of his life and took care of him," Brandstatter said. "Bennie was cremated, and nobody in the family claimed the ashes; there was some estrangement or something. So somebody at the funeral home called and asked Ron if he wanted the ashes. He picked them up and took the ashes in a cardboard box to a bar.

"Kramer told himself, 'What am I going to do?' He told the bartender, 'Pour me a beer and pour him a bourbon and water.' The bartender said, 'Who's the bourbon and water for?' Kramer told him, 'The guy in the box.' And after leaving the bar, Kramer had it figured out.

"He walked to Ferry Field, where Bennie played, and spread some ashes there. Then he did the same thing at Oosterbaan Field House and the golf course where the team used to stay the night before games. And then he went to the tunnel of the football stadium and spread what was left of the ashes. When he was done with that, Ron said, 'Bennie is gone.'"

Brandstatter said Michigan athletic administrator Fritz Seyferth, his former teammate, and longtime Michigan football equipment manager, Jon Falk, verified the story.

Football at Michigan is a family affair for those who have been together for decades through joy and heartache. And it has been a football family that even takes in a stray Buckeye or two. Remember that Bo was once an assistant football coach in Columbus.

And there was Robbie, whose favorite colors went from Scarlet and Gray to Maize and Blue. Brandy said it was Bo who won her over on the Wolverines.

"She appreciated that Bo was kind to Woody after the Clemson incident [Hayes punched Clemson linebacker Charlie Bauman in the 1978 Gator Bowl] that cost him his job," Brandstatter said. "And we did a lot of things socially with Bo and [his wife] Millie.

"She's more of a Michigan fan than an Ohio State fan these days. Robbie still likes them a little bit, but she no longer worships the Evil Empire."

FRANK BECKMANN

Frank Beckmann and Jim Brandstatter were asked individually for their favorite moment in more than three decades of broadcasting Michigan football. Neither hesitated in their selection, and both chose the same one.

It came after cornerback Charles Woodson intercepted a pass by Ohio State quarterback Stanley Jackson in the end zone for a touchback in the 1997 game. They were standing in their broadcast booth just north of the 50-yard line in the third quarter, windows open in order to experience the same elements the players had. It was snowing and raining during that game, and there was a stiff 10-mph northwest wind.

But they'd both just seen something that warmed their hearts.

"We were rocking back and forth up there because it had become such a tense game," Beckmann said. "And when Woodson picked off that ball in the end zone, I said, 'Polish up the trophy! Clear off the mantel! And make room for the Heisman Trophy!'"

Brandstatter smiled and stepped back in the booth.

"I'm watching Frank go into this soliloquy about Woodson," Brandstatter said, "and he's pointing down at the field over and over. I just applauded and didn't say a thing. It was that good. It doesn't get any better than that, when a guy has just the right emotion to match the moment."

Woodson had already returned a punt 78 yards for a touchdown and caught a 37-yard pass from Brian Griese to key a scoring drive. He had made big plays on special teams, offense, and now defense.

"That's the one call I will always remember," Beckmann said. "I do not know how I can beat that one."

There is magic in the radio booth when the knowledge, skill, and respect of a broadcast duo comes through at such a moment.

Beckmann said that during that game he had a flashback to 1991 and working with another former Wolverine as his partner. Bob Thornbladh, who was a running back and an assistant coach under Bo Schembechler, was working in the booth with Beckmann when Desmond Howard had his 93-yard punt return touchdown against Ohio State in Ann Arbor.

Beckmann said, "Thornbladh watched the play conclude and said, 'That's the Heisman Trophy winner!' I was more in tune, thinking back to that and thinking ahead to be ready if something like that happened again."

He said the key is being both prepared and maintaining spontaneity. "There's no script," Beckmann said. "You just describe what you see and describe what you feel. The goal Brandy and I have in the booth is simple. We are two guys sitting at barstools and talking about a game. And we have a saying: 'Check your ego at the door.'"

They did Michigan games together for several years in the 1980s and have been a team on WJR games since 1996. They also did Detroit Lions games together, and Beckmann had a stint doing the Detroit Tigers.

"It's almost indescribable to be calling games with one of my best friends," Beckmann said. "I have a passion for Michigan football, but Jim's exceeds mine. He played here and just loves everything about it.

"Jim never takes a game off, never mails it in, and is always impeccably prepared. We play off each other well and make fun of one another's shortcomings. He's the best partner I've had in any sport—a delight."

The Big House becomes their office on a half dozen Saturdays each autumn. "When I walk down the tunnel onto the field, I still get—not chills—but close to it," Beckmann said. "I think of all the great players who have run down that tunnel. And I love to get up in the booth and look over the rim of the stadium at Ann Arbor and all the trees changing colors; it's a real color tour. It's just a comfort, so relaxing.

"It's really not like work up there, and it's become a second home to me. There is this sea of humanity in the stadium that just comes alive. Keith Jackson started calling it the 'Big House,' and it's the perfect name for it. And then the players run out under the M Club banner. I always anticipate that, never get tired of that."

Thirty-two years of soaking in the sights, sounds, and smells of Michigan football have left memories he cherishes as much as watching the playmakers from Anthony Carter to Denard Robinson dazzle the crowds.

But Beckmann recalled his "inauspicious" beginning in 1981. He was replacing the legendary Bob Ufer, who had died of cancer that season. Michigan was ranked No. 1 but lost the opener 21–14 at Wisconsin. And Bo put Beckmann on the spot in their first meeting.

Beckmann was an investigative reporter at WJR until switching to the sports department in 1981. Bob Page, a fixture at the state's most powerful radio station, took him to meet the football coach in Ann Arbor.

"We went into the coaches' locker room after the game," Beckmann said. "It was a small room, and everyone was jammed in tight. I extended my hand to Bo, and we shook. And then he said, 'Beckmann, huh? You're the investigative reporter.' I said, 'Yes, I am, sir.'

"Bo looked me in the eye and said, 'There's nothing to investigate here, got it?'"

Beckmann chuckled and added, "I didn't know what to think after that. But we became great friends. I'd watch film with Bo Schembechler. He would smoke his pipe, and I would light up a cigarette. And we'd talk about everything."

Beckmann didn't usually fly with the team, but he did on a 1983 trip to Seattle for a game with the University of Washington. He had just received a death threat in the mail, which he reported to the proper authorities. His wife, Karen, was eight months pregnant with their first child, and he was on pins and needles.

"I did not tell anybody about it except Brandy," Beckmann said. "The guy who wrote the letter was upset over the way I was calling Michigan games. He said I made every excuse in the book for the Lions but was too critical of Michigan. He wrote, 'If I don't like the way you call this game, I'll kill you.'"

The Wolverines lost 25–24, and it wasn't the kind of game to make an edgy fan happy.

Beckmann paced nervously on the plane ride back to Detroit after the game.

Beckmann said, "Bo saw me and said, 'What's the matter, Beckmann?' I told him the story and he said, 'Ahh, it's just some crackpot. Don't even think about it.'"

After getting their luggage at Metro Airport, Bo, Brandstatter, and Beckmann walked to their cars in the multi-leveled parking structure. It was early Sunday morning, still and quiet. Beckmann bid them good-bye and walked toward his car. But Bo could sense his uneasiness and doubled back.

"I looked back, and there was Bo," Beckmann said. "He said, 'Where's your car, Beckmann?' We walked to it, and he stood there until I got in my car and left. Next week, after the game, I thanked him for doing that. Bo said, 'Beckmann, no one's going to get you as long as I'm around here.'"

TOM HEMINGWAY

Listening to Tom Hemingway on the radio was like having a friend who shared the experience of a Michigan football game with you. With sharp descriptions, he painted a picture in your mind of what was happening on the field, and he wove in the stories of the players and coaches at just the right times.

Hemingway was the radio voice to take along with you on a drive through the country or to sit with you on your front porch swing. His deep baritone voice was soothing and reassuring. You got all the facts from Hemingway because he was a strong reporter, but he also had a feel for the rhythm of the game. While many announcers are best appreciated in quick bursts of brilliance, his strength was the consistency of his entire body of work.

He did Wolverines football games from 1963 to 2000 with one short break when campus station WUOM wasn't allowed to carry games because of an exclusivity clause in the broadcast contract of WJR in Detroit. He also did Michigan basketball and baseball games and authored a book in 1985, *Life Among the Wolverines*.

Hemingway's longtime broadcast partner was former Michigan quarterback Tom Slade. Shawn Hemingway, his son, served as their spotter in the broadcast booth for many years. Now, Tom Hemingway is the only one of the trio left, having buried both a beloved son and a cherished friend.

When Slade died of leukemia on November 15, 2006, Hemingway flew in for the funeral from his home in Tucson, Arizona. Shawn joined him at the church in Ann Arbor.

"I was coming in the back door of the church along with Shawn for Tom's funeral," Hemingway said. "And Bo and his wife [Cathy] were coming in the same hallway. Bo stopped when he saw me and had a nice conversation with me and Shawn. He could not have been nicer to my son."

Bo developed a special friendship with Slade, who was also his dentist. When his old coach visited Slade in the hospital in his final days, Slade fell asleep. He awoke five hours later to find Bo sitting in the same chair, waiting to be there for him when his eyes opened. On the same Thursday night of Slade's funeral, Bo addressed the Michigan football team before its battle for No. 1 with Ohio State in Columbus. His speech detailed what went into being a "Michigan Man," and how Slade filled that description as well as anyone ever had.

He was Bo's quarterback on a 1971 team that was undefeated in 11 games before losing to Stanford 13–12 in the 1972 Rose Bowl. But he became so much more to the coach than an option wizard who never backed down on plays.

"A lot of people considered Bo to be a hard, gruff, mean person," Hemingway said. "But that wasn't Bo. He was someone who truly cared for people."

The day after Slade's funeral, Shawn called his father.

"Hey, Dad, did you hear about Bo?'" Shawn asked.

"No," replied his father.

Shawn took a deep breath and added, "He's gone."

It was a week that left the Hemingways and countless Michigan fans dazed, heads spinning.

Shawn died of brain cancer in 2012, and the loss has been difficult for Hemingway and his wife, Jenne. But the father often smiles when thinking about the time he spent with his son and Slade on Michigan football Saturdays.

"Tom Slade was a great, great partner and a very, very close friend," Hemingway said. "No. 1, Tom had a great sense of humor. I think every play-by-play guy likes a color man who would mess with him. And I needed the help that way from a guy like Tom.

"He never let the fact that he'd been a Michigan quarterback affect his criticism during games. And his great stories of his playing days and Bo were a great way of framing it. I found myself just listening to him sometimes. And then I'd catch myself, and say, 'Wow, it's my turn.'"

They covered the 1985 game between No. 1 Iowa and No. 2 Michigan in Iowa City on the roof of the Kinnick Stadium press box in an auxiliary booth. The tremendous demand for media credentials and broadcast booths for the biggest national game of the year brought about the roof assignment.

"There was only room for Tom and I in there," Hemingway said. "Our engineer had to sit in a chair outside the booth. You get involved in the game and don't consider your surroundings as much. But it was different, not fun."

Hemingway chuckled, recalling the cramped quarters from which he watched and called the Rob Houghtlin chip-shot field goal that made Iowa a 12–10 winner on the game's final play.

There were plenty of big games for Hemingway in more than 30 years of calling Wolverines football, and he was the only announcer to call the three biggest wins the team has claimed in the last half century: the 1969 upset of Ohio State, the 1997 win over Ohio State, and the Rose Bowl win over Washington State that culminated that undefeated season.

"For me," Hemingway said, "it's the '69 Ohio State game. You still can't top that one. Ohio State was more than the No. 1 college team. There were actually discussions that year about how they'd fare against NFL teams.

"There was this feeling of disbelief as the game was ending, 'Is this actually happening?' At the end, I simply said, 'And the unbelievable has taken place.'"

Hemingway also called one of the most outstanding, and yet over-looked, performances in Michigan history: Ron Johnson's 347 yards and five touchdowns rushing—both still school records—against Wisconsin in Ann Arbor on November 16, 1968.

"It was a terrible day weather-wise," Hemingway said. "There was rain and snow. It was cold, wet, and windy. And the stands were half-empty. It took a few years to get the place full. Ron was just so elusive. Then you combine that with his power, and you had a runner eluding defenders and bouncing off them.

"I remember that determination—that second drive he had that day. He reminded me an awful lot of Tshimanga Biakabutuka."

Biakabutuka's 313 yards rushing against Ohio State in 1995 ranks second on the school's rushing honor roll, and Hemingway called that game, too.

The most exciting Wolverine in Tom's book was Anthony Carter.

"You could not take your eyes off of Anthony," Hemingway said. "And when the ball was thrown to him, you did not say 'incomplete' until you saw the ball on the ground. He made catches that I could not believe."

Hemingway admired the resiliency of option quarterback Rick Leach for "the pounding he took" on play after play over the course of four seasons, and he said Desmond Howard made you feel "like he would score even before he got the ball."

He said Charles Woodson was close to Carter in regard to "capturing your attention," and he described tailback Gordon Bell as "a water bug who disappeared in a pile and squirted out the other end."

Hemingway grew up in tiny Wacousta, Michigan, listening to Ty Tyson broadcasting Michigan football when Fritz Crisler was coaching the Wolverines to Big Ten and national championships.

"When I started broadcasting at Michigan Stadium," Hemingway said, "I had just total wonderment. I thought, 'My gosh, I'm going to be broadcasting here.' I was so steeped in the Michigan football lore."

And over the next 40 years, Hemingway both described and became a part of that lore.

DID YOU KNOW?

Hemingway never brought up his famous novelist relative while we were covering Michigan football together. But years later, while we were both living in Tampa Bay, I asked Tom if he was related to Ernest Hemingway and received a surprise affirmative answer.

"He's a distant cousin," Tom said. "We can nail it down to being a third cousin, twice removed. That's not as close as my dad would've liked it to be."

CHAPTER 5

Jim Harbaugh Guaranteed

Jim Harbaugh was in his office early one morning in 2013 at the San Francisco 49ers complex in Santa Clara, California, watching videotape of his latest successor as the Michigan quarterback, Denard Robinson. Harbaugh was taken not only by the dazzling athlete on the field, but by the overall scene inside and outside the Big House. At that instant, he took my phone number out of his pocket and called it.

"I've been meaning to call you for a week, Steve," he said, "and I'm sorry about the delay. But I've got Michigan Stadium, as big as life, up on the screen in my office right now. I knew I had to call you.

"I'm watching Denard Robinson, and he's amazing. But I'm finding myself looking around the whole stadium and at the scoreboard, and the trees beyond the stadium and the golf course in the distance. It's all such a special place."

Harbaugh grew up about one mile from Michigan Stadium while attending elementary, middle, and high schools in Ann Arbor in the 1970s, when his father, Jack, was an assistant coach for the Wolverines. Then Jim quarterbacked the team from 1984–86, developing into an NFL first-round pick. He had a long and successful playing career before getting into coaching and becoming the head coach at Stanford before landing the Niners job and leading them to the Super Bowl in his second season as their head coach.

It's been quite a ride, going from shagging balls on the Michigan sideline and trying to stay out of Bo Schembechler's hair to coaching in pro football's mega-game—against his older brother, John, no less.

But along the way, he's never lost his attachment to the Wolverines, their tradition, and their legendary coach. There was a flap in 2007 when he made some comments critical of the academics at his alma mater. But his love for all things Maize and Blue endures.

Harbaugh said, "Michigan is a part of my life—from my childhood to my high school years to my college years. We moved a lot with my dad changing schools all the time, and I don't know if I ever considered any place to be my hometown. But I guess I do consider Ann Arbor my hometown.

"Michigan will always have a special place in my heart. It helped prepare me for the job I'm in now. And this is the biggest challenge of my life."

I assumed that the challenge he spoke of was winning the Super Bowl, which he'd lost 34–31 two months earlier to the Baltimore Ravens.

"No," Harbaugh said, "just winning the next game is the biggest challenge. And I know that I've found what I love and that I'm blessed to coach. I love this challenge."

Harbaugh said he learned the essence of success at Michigan. "The lessons I learned there had to do with team effort and individual effort," he said. "I learned that if you have a good attitude and work hard, you can't help but be successful. Guys who do not work hard and do not have a good attitude, it's impossible for them to succeed. I saw that clearly.

"I was showered with that daily by Bo Schembechler: 'Work hard!' I learned of the cause we were fighting for all through summer, spring, and winter conditioning.... And through two-a-day practices and all the fall practices."

I asked for a specific example of a lesson learned from Bo. "Oh, man," Harbaugh said. "There are so many, hundreds. But for me it was the daily kinds of things. I look at Bo and the greatest thing, what I love

Head coach Bo Schembechler yells at quarterback Jim Harbaugh as the Wolverines fell victim to Arizona State 22-15 in the Rose Bowl in Pasadena, California, on January 1, 1987. For Schembechler, it was his seventh loss in Rose Bowl action. (AP Photo/Reed Saxon)

about him, is that he took the game very seriously but not himself.

"One day, he was wearing that tight, scrunched-down hat, shorts, and a T-shirt with white socks and his coaching shoes. I said, 'Going for a workout, Bo?' He said, 'Yeah, I've got to work out, Jim. You are looking at the world's most perfectly figured man.' And he'd swell up his chest and stick it out. I couldn't stop laughing.

"But he said things like that all the time. With most people, you say, 'How you doing?' And they say, 'Good.' You say, 'How's the family?' And they say, 'Good.' And you are past them and nothing happens. But Bo had a way of making every moment exciting. One time, when I was 9 or 10, he looked at me and said, 'Jimmy, did I ever tell you about the time I was a great pitcher at Barberton [Ohio] High School, a fire-balling left-hander?'"

Harbaugh chuckled and groaned. And by the way, he does a great

Bo impersonation. Whenever he quoted Bo, he did so in his mentor's gruff yet somehow loving tone.

Bo has stayed in his head and his heart all these years.

On the shelf next to the desk in his office, Harbaugh has three autographed photos. One is of President Ronald Reagan, another is of his brother, John, and the other is of Bo.

"It's a picture of me and Bo at the Rose Bowl," Harbaugh said. "We're on the sideline, and he has his left hand on his head set and the fingers of his right hand are curled around the collar of my jersey. He signed it, 'To Jim: A great quarterback.... A good friend. Best Wishes, Bo Schembechler.'"

Playing for Bo was, quite simply, the best.

I recalled that photo as he described it, and it took me back in time.

Ann Arbor was and remains like most college towns. Students rent out rooms in what were once large, single-family homes. They generally are let go by landlords, littered by the students with McDonald's bags and bottles, and decorated with posters of rock stars and swimsuit models.

Harbaugh and Andy Moeller lived in one of those places in the summer of 1985. I visited them before two-a-day practices began to interview Harbaugh, and the three of us sat on the porch and talked for a while first. It wasn't much of a place, but it was close to Harbaugh's favorite eatery, Blimpy Burger—where you could get a fried egg on the burger and the best onion rings on the planet.

Harbaugh and Moeller noted that I had been pretty hard on them in my *Ann Arbor News* columns the year before, trying to get a rise out of me.

"You guys were 6–6 last year," I said. "What did you want me to write? That this is a great Michigan team even though it lost more games in one year than Bo usually takes three or four years to lose?"

They shrugged their shoulders and began to understand that the media isn't necessarily out to get them. For the most part, you take heat when you lose and credit when you win.

And Harbaugh would get plenty of credit before taking off the winged helmet for the last time. He led Michigan to a final No. 2 ranking in 1985 and a Big Ten championship in 1986 when he was the Big Ten's Most Valuable Player and finished third in the Heisman Trophy voting.

The Wolverines were so close to the Holy Grail of college football in Harbaugh's senior season. They were undefeated and No. 2 in 1986 and on the verge of perfection and a possible national championship. However, it all went up in smoke with a 20–17 loss to Minnesota in the Big House.

So when Harbaugh spoke to reporters two days later and five days before playing the Buckeyes, he dropped a bomb of a prediction: "I guarantee we will beat Ohio State and be in Pasadena New Year's Day. People might not give us a snowball's chance in hell to beat them in Columbus, but we're going to. We don't care where we play the game. I hate to say it, but we could play at noon or midnight. We're going to be jacked up, and we're going to win."

What in the world was Bo going to say about this? He hated braggadocio—especially when it fired up an opponent. But when he was asked about it that Monday at the Weber's Inn luncheon, he surprised everybody. He said he wouldn't want a quarterback who would think otherwise and completely defused the coach-quarterback controversy that everyone anticipated. And it might have been one of the smartest things Bo ever did. It sent the Wolverines into that game with a swagger that was unique for a program that stressed doing its talking on the field.

Bo didn't like it, for sure. But he said and did what was best for a unified front.

"I didn't know what Bo would say about it," Harbaugh said all these years later. "But from the time I was a little kid, I wanted to play in the Rose Bowl. I saw it as my destiny. I went to three Rose Bowls and walked the sideline as a kid. Michigan needed to win that game to get there, and it was my last chance—the last chance for a lot of us. We had to win, and that's how I felt about it.

"Bo pulled me into the area where the coaches dress for practice that Monday, and he reacted a lot better than I expected. He looked at me and said, 'Well, you shot your mouth off again.' I said, 'Yes, I did.' And then he just said, 'Well, we're going to have to back it up for you.' And then, in front of the team, Bo said, 'I know one guy who thinks we can win this game, and that's our quarterback!'

"He had my back, and that felt so good."

Michigan won 26–24 when Buckeyes placekicker Matt Frantz hooked a 45-yard field-goal attempt to the left with 1:06 to play in the Horseshoe. Harbaugh's guaranteed win over Ohio State, in which he threw for 261 yards and Jamie Morris ran for 210 yards and two touchdowns, allowed Bo's mantra to hold true: "Those Who Stay Will Be Champions."

Had the Wolverines lost that game and the Rose Bowl berth, they also would have lost the Big Ten championship. And for the first and only time, players who spent four years in Bo's program would have been denied a conference championship ring and a trip to Pasadena.

Morris and the offensive line, led by All-American offensive tackle John "Jumbo" Elliott, did more to win the showdown. However, it was going to be remembered as Harbaugh's game. Win, lose, or draw, it didn't matter. The Michigan quarterback was going to be the braggart who couldn't deliver the goods or the cocky kid who made good on his promise.

Buckeyes fans spewed obscene chants his way that Saturday, and it wasn't exactly a welcome mat that he received in Ann Arbor that week.

"Everyone outside the team hooted on me and compared me to Antoine Joubert," Harbaugh told me after the game, referring to the Wolverines basketball player who predicted a win over Michigan State and ate crow. "The students on campus said I was cocky, arrogant.

"And it fired up the fans here at Ohio State. They chanted, 'Harbaugh (blanks)! Harbaugh (blanks)! But that just had us jacked up."

He might not have scored or thrown a touchdown in this monumental game, but Harbaugh led his team to victory and showed plenty of moxie.

Buckeyes coach Earle Bruce was upset that game officials took away one of OSU's timeouts when they decided the Ohio Stadium crowd was too loud for Michigan's offense to hear its signals.

Asked if he blamed the officials for taking the crowd out of the game, Bruce at first said yes. Then he paused, adding, "Let me correct that. Mr. [Jim] Harbaugh took the crowd out. He was the official."

Running off the field after the final gun with the scarlet and gray throng now silenced by defeat, Harbaugh experienced a sense of supreme satisfaction that extended to his family.

"As I ran off," he said, "I saw the smiling faces of my dad, mom, and family. That's something I'll never forget."

It was the end of a trying, anxious week for the Harbaughs. The quarterback's father had just been fired as the head coach at Western Michigan, where his brother, John, was also on the coaching staff and subsequently let go. But both Jack and John were beaming when I ran into them as we all headed toward the Michigan locker room. The pain of losing their jobs was dulled for a few glorious hours.

After three Greyhound Americruisers carrying the Wolverines departed for the airport, I asked Jack and John what Jim's accomplishment meant to them.

"I was thrilled for Jim," John said. "That guarantee quote was no surprise to me. People said it was out of character. But he wasn't cocky and was right in character. Ever since Jim was 10 years old, he said he was going to take Michigan to the Rose Bowl."

Plenty of kids growing up in Michigan fantasize about doing just that, but Jim got to experience the granddaddy of them all firsthand. His hero was All-American quarterback Rick Leach, who gave him wristbands and caused him to dream big dreams. And Jim would end up breaking many of Leach's records and playing in the Rose Bowl just like Leach.

Jack recalled, "Our first Rose Bowl trip was in 1977. We went three straight years after winning those Big Ten titles [in 1976, 1977, and 1978]. Jim and Andy Moeller went to all three, but this was their last chance to go as players.

"I'll never forget the day he came into our room after that first game and said, 'Dad, I want to be on the field in the Rose Bowl some day when the sun drops behind the [San Gabriel] mountains in the second half.'"

Did he predict a Rose Bowl win as a young boy?

"No," Jack said, pausing to chuckle. "No, he didn't. But wait until the week before this Rose Bowl."

Jim made no such prediction in Pasadena, and Michigan lost 22–15 despite taking a 15–3 lead on Arizona State on Harbaugh's two-yard touchdown run. But Harbaugh threw three interceptions, and the Wolverines were held scoreless in the second half.

So in a season where the Rose Bowl was the team's driving force, simply getting there is most remembered. Anticipation often proves to be the greater joy, and nothing that year would top the triumph in Columbus.

"I watched to see what Jimmy would do after the game," his father said. "He picked up the ball and walked off the field shaking it. That's when I had a flashback to that talk in our room. He's a special kid—a special kid."

Jim Harbaugh and Moeller, who made 13 tackles against the Buckeyes, also wanted to beat Ohio State to get Bo the 166th victory that moved him ahead of Fielding H. Yost on the all-time Michigan list. Doing so would allow Harbaugh and Moeller the opportunity to deliver Bo the plaque they purchased to commemorate that milestone by passing the hat among teammates.

"We chipped in to get a nice plaque," Harbaugh said. "It cost about $200, and we had it engraved for a win over Minnesota [which turned out to be that 20–17 upset loss]. It cost us 30 bucks to get the inscription changed on it. The big joke on the team was that we could not afford to lose this game."

Moeller added, "It was better to give it to Bo down here at Ohio State anyway."

They headed out of the stadium together, their Rose Bowl dream about to be realized by winning the Big Ten title in their final chance.

"Guarantee 'em all, Jimmy," Moeller said.

Harbaugh laughed.

As the lifelong friends boarded the victory bus, I had a flashback to that talk the three of us had on the porch of their Ann Arbor rental house after coming off a dreadful season two years earlier. The determination I sensed then had carried them to their goal.

When we were done talking that day, Harbaugh walked to the street with me toward our cars. He had an old red Volkswagen Beetle that sometimes had to be push-started, and he laughed about what a "crappy car" he had. After the Chicago Bears selected him and he went from Bo to Mike Ditka, I asked him about being able to afford some decent wheels and getting rid of his VW.

"Oh," Harbaugh said, "I don't even have that bomb anymore. I couldn't keep the inside of the windshield from icing over, and I just abandoned it on one of the streets last winter."

When we talked on the phone, he laughed about that red bug and Harbaugh said, "Do you remember the shifter on it? I drilled a hole into a baseball and stuck it on the shifter knob."

Some perceived Jim Harbaugh as privileged, but he really wasn't. While his father did get his foot in the door, it was the son who kicked the door down and established a legacy as not only a game-changer but a program-changer.

The Wolverines accomplished more than going 21–3–1 in Harbaugh's last two seasons. They turned an important page as he became Bo's one and only NFL draft first-round-pick quarterback, opening the gates for an entirely different brand of football.

It was Harbaugh who changed the three-yards-and-a-cloud-of-dust culture at Michigan. He turned it into a school that passing quarter-backs would not only consider, but choose. Harbaugh begat Elvis Grbac, who begat Todd Collins, who begat Scott Dreisbach and Brian Griese, who begat Tom Brady and Drew Henson, who begat John Navarre, who begat Chad Henne. That's nine NFL quarterbacks from the 1987 draft to the 2008 draft.

Grbac surpassed all of Harbaugh's career passing records. And so I asked Cam Cameron, the passing whiz who coached them both, who he would pick if he could only have one. He chose Harbaugh.

"Both were great," Cameron said. "But Elvis was working out of a true passing offense. Jimmy was still running the option and put up those numbers."

Harbaugh's 387 pass completions, 62.4 percent completion rate, and 5,449 passing yards all topped the school's career passing lists when he graduated. And he basically set those marks in two seasons by throwing for 2,729 yards as a senior and 1,976 as a junior. Steve Smith's 1,735 yards in 1982 had been the single-season record.

Despite being an accomplished quarterback at Ann Arbor Pioneer High and then Palo Alto (California) High, after his father became the defensive coordinator at Stanford, Harbaugh was not everybody's All-American. In fact, there were Michigan boosters who griped about giving Jack Harbaugh's kid a scholarship.

Jim visited schools where he knew the coaches through his father: Stanford, Arizona, Wisconsin, and Michigan. Cal-Berkeley was his only visit to a school without personal ties. In fact, the late Dave McClain, then the Badgers coach, was once his babysitter.

"I knew that Dave McClain thought a California quarterback would make his program," Harbaugh told me while playing at Michigan. "People think quarterbacks from California have an extra finger or something. But the seven-on-seven passing leagues they have there do make a difference. You play 20 games of touch football with nothing but throwing. They keep stats, and it's big like American Legion baseball is here. And I got to throw with John Elway, Steve Dils, and Turk Schonert to guys like Ken Margerum."

They all played for Stanford either before or while his father coached there, and Jim tried to emulate Elway, who shared quarterback pointers with Jim, then a three-sport star who also excelled in baseball and basketball. But he learned about something more important than spirals and reading a defense in Palo Alto.

"I always loved sports," Harbaugh told me while in college. "But I had no self-control until I got to Palo Alto. I got along better with the people out there because they are so easy-going. But I guess I grew up, too. I figured I couldn't act like a jerk because I wouldn't have any friends.

"I went to a high school there that was full of kids with a lot of money. Most of their parents were tied to Stanford in some way. They influenced me to do better in school. And I knew I couldn't go to a good school because my grades wouldn't be good enough."

In addition to the honors won strictly for football at Michigan, Harbaugh was also named to the Big Ten All-Academic team. And yet academics at his alma mater became the center of a controversy he prompted with negative comments about the general studies program at Michigan that he made to Pat Forde, who was then working for ESPN. Forde pointed out that, according to the Wolverines' 2007 media guide, only 30 football players listed majors, and 19 of those listed general studies as their major.

The fall-out was massive—with Harbaugh's former tailback Jamie Morris, then a Michigan athletic administrator, and Mike Hart, then the school's star tailback, firing back at Harbaugh.

"My motivation was positive," Harbaugh told Forde in 2007, before his first year as the Stanford coach. "I see how it's done now at Stanford, and I see no reason to believe it can't be the same there. I have a great love for Michigan and what it's done for me. Bo Schembechler was like a second father. Michigan is a great school and always has been, and I don't see why they can't hold themselves to a higher standard.

"Most college football fans, unfortunately, just think about how exciting it is to watch college players play and not about what happens when the football comes to a screeching halt. They need to get a degree— a quality degree—and develop a skill set that helps you for the next 60–70 years.

"There is no general studies at Stanford. In my opinion, that major does not give you the skill set to compete [in the business world]."

Lloyd Carr, entering his final season before retiring as the head coach, termed Harbaugh's comments "elitist," "arrogant," and "self-serving."

Hart told reporters that summer at a Big Ten media session in Chicago, "That's a guy I have no respect for. You graduate from the University of Michigan, and you're going to talk about your school like that, a great university like we have? To say that we're not true student-athletes? I don't know if maybe he wants to coach here and he's mad because he didn't get a job.... He's not a Michigan Man. I wish he'd never played here."

This all came down just months after Bo died.

"Mike Hart is just repeating their messages," Harbaugh told Forde. "When I was a player, there would have been nobody saying anything like what Mike Hart said about me. We would have been too afraid of the consequences. That wouldn't have happened while Bo was there."

When we talked from his office at the 49ers complex, I asked Harbaugh to explain and reflect on those comments and the feathers he'd ruffled six years prior.

"Forde was following up on something I told Glenn Dickey [of the *San Francisco Examiner*]," Harbaugh said. "And what I was saying was that if you let a college student get by on his athletic ability, you are cheating him. That was straight from Bo and Woody [Hayes], but I was not targeting Michigan. But I believe in those principles and will not back down from what I said."

Harbaugh said that he graduated from Michigan with a degree in communications in 1987.

His quote in Dickey's column was, "Michigan is a good school and I got a good education there, but the athletic department has ways to get borderline guys in and, when they're in, they steer them to courses in sports communications. They're adulated when they're playing, but when they get out, the people who adulated them won't hire them."

Harbaugh recalled that interview. "I had just become the coach at Stanford and talked to Glenn Dickey about everything, my whole upbringing and my love of Michigan," Harbaugh said. "Then, in the middle of that, we started talking about academics, and I'm trumpeting Stanford as a school and what it takes to get in. I said it was the finest education in college football. I said that not every school out there is doing that, and discussed the exceptions made for athletes by big-time programs. I said we did not cut those corners at Stanford. I noted that I got a great education at Michigan, and it got tied into a quote like I was specifically talking about Michigan.

"I thought it was unfair the way it was printed. It did ruffle a lot of feathers at Michigan, but I did not target Michigan specifically."

Months later, with Michigan shopping for a replacement for Carr, Harbaugh's name did not come to the forefront. Instead, former Wolverines player and assistant coach Les Miles, the LSU head coach known as "The Hat" for the Schembechler-like baseball cap he wears on the sideline, became the candidate many Wolverines fans coveted. Michigan ended up settling for West Virginia coach Rich Rodriguez, and the result was the lone losing coaching regime in program history. Rich Rod finished 15–22 before being replaced by Brady Hoke.

Harbaugh became the coach at Stanford exactly 25 years after graduating from Palo Alto High in 1982, and he led the Cardinals to a 12–1 season in 2010 capped by an Orange Bowl win over Virginia Tech. His star was rising, and there were those ready to forgive and forget to bring Harbaugh back to Michigan. Although there were others who were not in a forgiving mood about Harbaugh's academics comments.

Michigan athletic director Dave Brandon said Hoke was the only one offered the job, and Harbaugh left Stanford during that same time frame to become the coach in San Francisco, making the exact move legendary coach Bill Walsh made from that school to the 49ers in 1979. Harbaugh wouldn't have stayed at Michigan long even if he had returned. The NFL got into his blood during a 15-year career that saw him throw for 26,888 yards and 129 touchdowns. He was the runner-up NFL MVP in 1995 when he led the Indianapolis Colts to the AFC Championship Game and went to the Pro Bowl as the top-rated passer.

Harbaugh retired as a player after the 2001 season, and he served as the quarterbacks coach of the Oakland Raiders during the next two seasons.

Our paths crossed again on January 26, 2003, outside Qualcomm Stadium in San Diego after the Tampa Bay Bucs had crushed his Raiders 48–21 in Super Bowl XXXVII. I was the pro football editor for the *Tampa Tribune* and returning to the press box on the walkway around the stadium when I recognized a familiar face. Harbaugh was carrying a briefcase and heading to the bus.

He was dejected, but I got him to smile. I mentioned that the last time we were both in this stadium, then named for San Diego sportswriter Jack Murphy, was in December 1984 for the strangest Holiday Bowl ever. Brigham Young beat Michigan 24–17 to remain undefeated and win the national championship. The Cougars were bound to the Holiday Bowl as Western Athletic Conference champions. And with other top teams locked into New Year's Day games, the bowl committee figured Michigan was BYU's best opponent because of its tradition and ability to pull TV ratings.

Chris Zurbrugg was quarterbacking the Wolverines, and Harbaugh was on the sideline due to a broken humerus bone in his left arm suffered while diving for a fumble by Morris in the Michigan State game that finished his season. Michigan walked off with a 6–6 record and disappointment after that game with BYU.

"A long time ago, wasn't it?" Harbaugh said.

We chatted about our lives for about five minutes and had places to go.

Although Harbaugh, who Bo always hoped would someday coach the Wolverines, didn't end up back in Ann Arbor with that opening in 2011, the man who got the job was one of Jack Harbaugh's assistants at Western Michigan when his son was starring at Michigan.

Hoke, in a *Sports Illustrated* interview in 2012 with Dan Patrick, stressed that you do not mess with any of the Harbaughs. "Jackie, the mother, probably knows more [football] than any of them," Hoke said. "You didn't want one of your guys to mess up because you're going to get a finger in your chest [from Jackie]."

Harbaugh came from a long line of intense competitors. He recalled playing checkers with his grandmother at a family Christmas party. "I won and she tipped over the checkerboard," Harbaugh said.

The Harbaughs also had what Bo liked to term "moxie"—taking initiative with spirit and courage. Bo loved to tell the story of returning to his office after a practice only to find young Jimmy leaning back in Bo's office chair with his feet on the desk.

"How are *you*, Jim Harbaugh?" Bo bellowed, thinking he would scare the bee-jabbers out of the kid.

Young Harbaugh smiled, changed nothing he was doing, and said, "Fine. How are you, Bo?"

Years later, Bo loved to tell the story.

"I knew I had a future quarterback, a future leader, right then and there," Bo said. "That kid had moxie!"

But he would require some harnessing. "Harbaugh was an ornery little devil," Bo said. "He was a stubborn but playful kid who was always in the locker room or on the sidelines. He had a temper that he had to learn to control, though. We couldn't have a coach *and* a quarterback with a bad temper.

"But I knew the Harbaugh kid had a special flair for competing.

Most of the coaches who recruited him out of Palo Alto knew him as a kid. They knew he could be a leader, and that's why they went after Jim."

Harbaugh said he "didn't know how to take" Bo when he was a freshman in 1983. "Then I learned what has really become a cliché about Bo," Harbaugh said. "If he's not yelling at you, he's forgotten you. As a freshman, I thought he hated me and that I'd never play. But eventually I realized he just wanted me to get better."

Bo needed Harbaugh to perform to the utmost of his ability perhaps as much as any quarterback he ever coached. After the talented Steve Smith's college career concluded with the narrow Sugar Bowl loss following the 1983 season, Harbaugh was Bo's only hope at quarterback. Had Harbaugh not developed into a difference-maker, there was no way either of his backups, Zurbrugg or Russ Rein, would have filled that role. The talent drop-off after Harbaugh was right off a cliff.

The Wolverines would not have achieved great things in 1985 and 1986 without Harbaugh, who epitomized everything Bo loved in a player. He seemed like the perfect fit to someday sit behind the head coach's desk he once played behind as a boy. But it wasn't to be. And somehow that still seems strange to me. I told him that.

"I never really looked that far ahead," Harbaugh said. "I just do my job and worry about today. Bo taught me that: 'Do a real good job on the job you have.' Then everything takes care of itself."

That was Bo's message on networking. And Harbaugh has come far and fast as a coach as a result. Life has even come full circle, with his 23-year-old son, Jay, working on John's staff along with Jim's good buddy Andy Moeller, the Ravens offensive line coach.

"At the Super Bowl," Jim Harbaugh said, "I only had one moment when I reflected on all that. It was during the National Anthem, and there was my brother with his arm around his daughter. And there was Andy, and there was Jay. My son was a first-year intern-slash-weight room-slash-quality-control-slash-video-guy."

And so the family coaching tradition continues.

Jim Harbaugh is firmly established in the NFL and fast becoming one of the pro game's most formidable forces, a program-changer once again. His niche came in coaching, all right. It just came on Sundays.

CHAPTER 6

South Carolina Frenzy

The most frenzied opening moments of a Michigan game that I've seen did not occur in a game against Ohio State or a Rose Bowl. It did not happen at a Notre Dame, Michigan State, or Penn State game. It happened on September 21, 1985, at Williams-Brice Stadium in Columbia, South Carolina.

What began quietly as the teams huddled in contained areas just outside their locker rooms became such a commotion of humanity that the press box swayed. There was a fan-inflicted earthquake going on below.

The players on both teams bobbed up and down in anticipation of taking the field. And five minutes before kickoff, the Wolverines charged onto the field. They leaped and swung fists, and the cascading boos of University of South Carolina fans engulfed them.

The South Carolina band then quickly formed two long rows that lined the entrance for the Gamecocks' players. And once their visitors from the north were in place to witness, the band began playing the theme song of *2001: A Space Odyssey*.

The drums, brass, and woodwinds belted it out: "Boom-boom! Boom-Boom! Dun-dun!...Tahhh-Dahhh!"

It was time for the Gamecocks, dressed in bright red uniforms, to hit the stage. They sprinted past the band members and onto the green grass of the field to mob one another. The crowd noise grew to near deafening levels.

I'd seen the Rolling Stones at Cobo Arena in Detroit and The Who at the Pontiac Silverdome, and their wild, rollicking stage entries had nothing on this. Were they going to play "Jumpin' Jack Flash" or football?

The Wolverines were furious on their sideline. These kinds of entries were not yet popular in college football. The white smoke billowing out of pipes and the sounds hurricane-force winds blaring over the Orange Bowl sound system as the Miami Hurricanes took the field had not gained many followers at that point, and it was viewed as unsportsmanlike.

Was this a battle of the bands or what? And if so, where was the Michigan marching band?

"The whole bit backfired on them," Wolverines tailback Jamie Morris said. "It made us even more ready to play. We heard all of that 'boom-boom, dun-dun…tahhh-dahhh' stuff and got jacked. I thought, *Hey, bring them on*. A lot of guys were saying that. It got us geeked. We thought, *You're not going to do this to us*."

So the Wolverines used the pulsating strains of "Sprach Zarathustra" to their own advantage.

South Carolina's emotional high lasted exactly one play. Gamecock linebacker Carl Hill cracked tailback Thomas Wilcher and knocked off his helmet. Hill even knocked the chin strap off the helmet. Wilcher, now the coach at powerhouse Cass Tech High in Detroit, got up, fixed his helmet, and put it back on. Then he rushed for a game-high 104 yards and one touchdown.

The Gamecocks were three-point favorites in this game, but they scored just three points. Michigan pounded them 34–3.

This was a much happier ending for the Wolverines than their next dramatic helmet-clearing hit at the hands of a South Carolina defender. Gamecocks defensive end Jadeveon Clowney crushed Michigan tailback Vincent Smith in the 2013 Outback Bowl, causing him to lose not only his helmet but also the ball. Clowney also recovered the ball after what *Sports Illustrated* referred to as "the crunch seen 'round the Internet" to set up a touchdown as South Carolina came back to win, 33–28.

But a theatrical display followed by a sensational hit did not get the better of the Wolverines in that 1985 game in Columbia.

"We knew they would do all the fancy things when they came onto the field," Wolverines coach Bo Schembechler said. "So we tried to take them in stride. Scoring the first touchdown, though, was very big to take some of the crowd away.

"We didn't buckle under. Through all that jazz, we hung together and played. I really liked that."

This would not be a team that could be intimidated on the road. It only lost once away from the Big House—falling 12–10 at No. 1 Iowa—and finished No. 2 in 1985. And with the top scoring defense in the nation, the Wolverines allowed just one road touchdown all season—a meaningless one in a 48–7 win at Minnesota. They were not intimidated in Columbia, and that did much to prepare them for the challenges ahead on hostile turf.

CHAPTER 7

John Kolesar, Buckeye Killer

John Kolesar was the Buckeye Killer. He had a real knack of sticking the dagger in Ohio State, and twice he made the big plays that led the Wolverines to victories over the school from his home state. He grew up in Westlake, just west of Cleveland. But Michigan had one recruiting advantage for which the Buckeyes had no trump card. Bill Kolesar, John's father, was a Wolverines lineman in the mid-1950s and loved his school and team until the day he died.

In 1985, Ohio State had gained momentum on a fourth-and-15 pass from Jim Karsatos to future NFL star Cris Carter that covered 36 yards and ended up in the end zone. Michigan's lead had been cut to three points with 10:10 remaining.

When a team takes a chance like that and not only makes the first down but scores...well, there's a pretty uneasy feeling in the stomachs of their opponents and fans.

But 51 seconds later, Jim Harbaugh and Kolesar turned back the tide by making their own waves. Their big play was one that had disaster or delirium written all over it because it was such a bang-bang encounter. Ohio State safety Sonny Gordon blitzed, leaving cornerback William White on an island, matching up one-on-one with Kolesar. Harbaugh picked up the blitz and knew there would be a price to pay if he couldn't beat Gordon to the punch. Gordon crashed into Harbaugh's ribs the instant he released the ball, and Kolesar did his part by getting a couple of steps on White.

Harbaugh went flying along with the ball, and the crowd in the Big House gasped and wondered. Did the ball have enough on it? Was it on target?

Kolesar lost the ball in flight but found it just in time and caught it in stride for the 77-yard touchdown that completed the game's scoring.

"Their safety was looking Harbaugh in the face and knocked him on his butt," Michigan coach Bo Schembechler said. "But he hit Kolesar for the touchdown and dragged himself off the field."

Harbaugh recovered and said afterward, "It was called a 376 or post pattern, and when I saw [Gordon] step over, I knew we'd have man coverage. The fact that he delayed to disguise the blitz helped me get it off. I saw John catch it as I was falling down."

It was the second-longest completion in school history, trailing only Rick Leach's 83-yarder to Jim Smith against Purdue in 1975. Harbaugh's touch and Kolesar's ability to relocate and catch the ball made it all happen under the lights.

Kolesar credited a drill his eighth grade coach at Lee Burneson Junior High in Westlake taught him for making the grab. "I looked over my shoulder for the ball and was blinded for about three seconds by looking right up into the lights," Kolesar said. "I saw it released but didn't see it again until it was just coming down.

"My junior high coach, John Thompson, taught us to lay on the ground and throw the ball straight up. When it gets as high as it's going, you close your eyes and catch it without opening them. That's how I learned to make a catch once you lose the ball. Luckily, Jim put it right on the money."

Muscle memory drills paid off with the play of the game in a rivalry where touchdowns had been a precious commodity.

Michigan won 27–17 for its highest point total against OSU since Harry Truman was President. Scores were generally so low in "The Game" that between 1936 and 1987—despite the national championship teams and Heisman Trophy winners both programs had over those 52 years—each school could claim just three games in which it reached 30 points. Michigan's 58–6 win in 1946 was the last time it scored more.

Kolesar came in and went out with a bang against the Buckeyes in the 1988 game that began the upward scoring trend in the rivalry with a 34–31 Wolverines victory. He didn't match the four catches for 109 yards as a freshman but had three for 93 yards as a senior and added a game-changing kickoff return.

Kolesar covered all 100 yards in two plays in the final two minutes of the 1988 game at the Horseshoe in Columbus, and he saved Michigan from a devastating loss. The Wolverines had a 20–0 lead, lost it when Ohio State scored on each of its first four second-half possessions, got it back again on a Leroy Hoard touchdown run, and fell behind 31–27 when Bill Matlock punched back with a 16-yard touchdown and 2:02 left to play.

However, Kolesar responded by returning the ensuing kickoff 59 yards. He came out for one play and then caught a 41-yard touchdown pass from Demetrius Brown to win the game.

"I joked with him after that game," said Gary Moeller, then the offensive coordinator. "I told John, 'If you were in great shape, we wouldn't have needed to take you out for that one play.' I'll tell you, players like Kolesar make you good coaches."

Especially when the Buckeyes were across the line of scrimmage.

"This one tops everything," said Kolesar, whose 20-yard touchdown catch on fourth down with 50 seconds remaining beat Alabama in Tampa, Florida, in the 1988 Hall of Fame Bowl, now the Outback Bowl. "It's the culmination of my four years at Michigan. It seems like a fairytale."

The win also allowed the Wolverines to go to the Rose Bowl—where Bo would win for only the second time—as outright champions at 7–0–1 rather than having to share it with 6–1–1 Michigan State.

"Kolesar won the game for us," Bo said at the postgame press conference. "He really bailed us out. He's a game-breaking guy."

After the news conference, I caught up to Bo in the tiny coaches' locker room at Ohio Stadium. He was smiling without restraint. He had this way of breaking off smiles by clenching his teeth to abide by that coaching edict of "never getting too high" from the highs. But the press conference was over and he wasn't holding back any joy among the members of his coaching staff.

"What are you going to do next year without Kolesar?" I asked.

He chuckled. "I've got a feisty little devil to take his place named Desmond Howard. Wait until you see him!"

That "feisty little devil" won the 1991 Heisman Trophy.

Desmond had it all over Kolesar in terms of career statistics but had nothing on him in the Ohio State game. Desmond caught eight passes for 169 yards and one touchdown against the Buckeyes and, of course, had the signature play of his career with the 93-yard punt return touchdown that preceded his Heisman pose in the end zone in 1991.

When the *Detroit Free Press* had me pick a 10-year All-Star team that paralleled a 10-year Michigan State team from George Perles' first decade as the Spartans' head coach, picking two wide receivers was quite a chore.

But I chose Desmond and Kolesar from a field that included several other super receivers—Derrick Alexander, Greg McMurtry, Mercury Hayes, and Chris Calloway. You could win championships with any pair from that group, but I went with the two players with the best history of coming up big when it mattered most. They had great hands, feet, speed, concentration, and blocking ability.

After that All-Star team came out in print before the 1993 season, Kolesar's father called me to say thank you. He knew how stiff the competition was and that his son's 61 catches for 1,425 yards and 12 touchdowns was several hundred yards behind those of McMurtry (2,163), Howard (2,146), Hayes (2,144), and Alexander (1,977).

However, nobody got more per catch out of that group than Kolesar with a 23.4 average. Next was McMurtry (19.5), and he was followed by Hayes (17.3), Howard (16.0), and Alexander (15.8). Kolesar averaged roughly 4-to-8 yards more per catch than each of those contemporaries.

Both No. 40 (Kolesar) and No. 21 (Howard) were high school running backs, and Bo liked finding tailbacks with the hands to split wide. They knew how to block and get yards after contact.

"Kolesar is a deceptively fast kid with good hands," Bo told me during Kolesar's freshman season. "He's a competitive little devil."

Being a "little devil," as you're picking up, was a supreme compliment coming from Bo. He reserved that description for quick, cagey, playmakers. A big tailback who moved the chains by absorbing hits and dragging tacklers for extra yards was "a load" in the Bo vernacular. Leroy Hoard, the 1989 Rose Bowl MVP and a Kolesar teammate, was "a load," no doubt.

One type of player complements the other because giving defenses a number of varied styles to contend with increases the odds for an offense to succeed. Do you use a safety to double-cover a "competitive little devil" on a passing route or allow that safety to plug a lane and key in on keeping "a load" from turning four-yard gains into 10-yarders? It's called choosing your poison.

Bo continued talking about what he saw in Kolesar while in high school, saying, "But he never played wide receiver. He was a high school running back, but I figured he'd be a defensive back. Then I saw how fast he was and those nice, soft hands. It would've been a shame not to use him."

Kolesar went from fourth string to first string as a freshman. He became the third-string flanker after starter Erik Campbell was hurt in the opener with Notre Dame. And then he beat out Gilvanni Johnson and Ken Higgins.

Kolesar was a solid, 6' and 190 pounds. He could bust tackles, but he also ran 40 yards in a speedy 4.3 seconds. And he could do two-handed basketball dunks with such force that he broke both arms dunking as a senior forward-center at Westlake High. Kolesar was in a pair of arm casts running from wrists to biceps when he signed a national letter of intent with Michigan that February.

"I was in the casts for six weeks," Kolesar said, "and the letter of intent I signed looked like a first grader's scratch."

But he was healed in plenty of time for practices that August in Ann Arbor. Despite the speed and hands, it was his blocking that got him moving up the depth chart all the way to the top.

Kolesar took visits to Ohio State, North Carolina, and Miami of Ohio—where his brother, Doug, was a punter. But there was little question as to where John would end up. He wanted to continue the Michigan Man legacy started by his father, a two-way tackle at Michigan who lettered in 1953–55 on teams that went a combined 19–8 for Wolverines coach Bennie Oosterbaan.

After Kolesar turned heads by making four catches for 148 yards against Purdue as a freshman in 1985, the late Bill Kolesar beamed with pride and told me, "Now John understands what I told him about how he would feel running out of the tunnel. But watching him do this in a game is unbelievable. I'm pinching myself."

Freshmen weren't eligible in the era when Bill played. He proceeded to tell me about how he had to wait in line before getting his chance as a senior and then ripped up his knee in the second game of that season against Michigan State.

"I played left tackle, and Ron Kramer was the left end," Bill said. "We worked together."

Kramer, a two-time All-America selection, is considered by many to be the best all-around athlete to ever wear the Maize and Blue in Ann Arbor. Kramer caught, threw, and ran the ball—and he was a devastating blocker. He also punted and handled the place-kicking. Kramer went on to become an All-Pro tight end in the NFL with the Green Bay Packers and Detroit Lions.

While at Michigan, Kramer won nine varsity letters—three each in football, track, and basketball. He led the football and basketball team in scoring. That would have been like Desmond scoring 15 to 20 points a game in basketball for the Wolverines. Or it would have been like Glen Rice of the 1989 national championship basketball team also scoring double-digit touchdowns as a receiver. And Kramer was a high-jumper in track. He weighed 230 pounds and could high jump 6'4".

John Kolesar had strong college football bloodlines on his mother, Joyce's, side of the family, as well. He is related to Charley Trippi, a two-time Georgia All-American back who led the Chicago Cardinals to the 1947 NFL championship and was inducted into the Pro Football Hall of Fame in 1968.

Kolesar grew up idolizing Anthony Carter, Michigan's three-time All-America receiver from 1980–82.

"When I was in the ninth grade, we used to play Sunday pickup games at the high school," Kolesar said. "I used to have two plays—A.C. right and A.C. left."

So it was a high compliment when Michigan's All-American quarterback Jim Harbaugh, now the coach of the San Francisco 49ers, said of Kolesar, "He's the closest thing we've had with speed to Anthony Carter."

Kolesar never had the chance to do damage in the NFL with the Buffalo Bills, who drafted him in the fourth round in 1989. He injured his knee and never played a down of pro football.

"John Kolesar was a competitor," Moeller said. "It's too bad he didn't get to play in the NFL because he would've been a slot receiver like Wes Welker."

Today, Kolesar is working in sales management and living in his hometown of Westlake.

There are players who surpassed his numbers and won more honors. But John Kolesar did two things that matter most at Michigan. He beat the Buckeyes and carried on the school's special traditions learned from his father.

CHAPTER 8

Adventures with Mark Messner

Every summer, I tried to visit the home or special place of a Michigan football player entering his senior year. It was my way of taking readers on a unique day trip with one of their favorite Wolverines and showing a special side of his life or interests.

Each of those days was a joy because I would discover what made their hearts beat the loudest, and I would meet the family and friends they had talked about for the past several years.

Mark Messner, who earned his second consensus All-American honor and became the school's first four-time All-Big Ten first-team selection for a Big Ten championship team, took me sailing on Lake Erie a few days before the demanding, draining practices began for the 1988 season. Michigan placekicker and good friend Mike Gillette, *Ann Arbor News* photographer Colleen Fitzgerald, Messner's father, and several others boarded the sailboat with us at a marina near Monroe, Michigan.

Being on a 44' sailboat and gliding with the wind has a way of shifting reality. The horizon is so far away that it welcomes the notion that an endless summer really is possible. But the two-a-day practices looming later in the week were a contrast to the peaceful water that Messner and Gillette were all too aware of as they pulled away from the dock.

"You go from the relaxing life of golf and sailing to the obnoxious aggression and down-n-dirty world of football," Messner said. "That's about the whole spectrum.

All-American tackle Mark Messner jokes with teammates during a work-out as the Wolverines held their first practice at Orange Coast Community College on Tuesday, December 27, 1988. Messner and the No. 11-ranked Michigan team took on fifth-ranked Southern California in the Rose Bowl on January 2, 1989. (AP Photo/Bob Galbraith)

"I'm a different person on the field. I'm at work then. It's two different worlds. But you have to separate yourself for both. People who can't do that become the stereotyped football player. I hate that image."

Messner never sits long enough to be labeled. He's driving across Ann Arbor to rent a Macintosh computer for a business class analysis. Or going through one of those grueling, two-hour off-season workouts. Or rushing to the airport to pick up a friend. Or headed for the links or the lake.

"I cannot stand to just pass time," Messner said. "One day, all I did was lift and hang out. It was such a long, long day. I wasn't cut out to be a couch potato."

On this particular day, Messner was sailing on *Outrageous*, a pleasure craft owned by his friend, Dr. Stanley Poleck. Nearly a dozen family members and friends were aboard, including Messner's father, Del Pretty.

They gathered at the Toledo Beach Marina for a three-hour spin on the western edge of Lake Erie. The temperature reached 95 degrees, and the deck became hotter as late morning gave way to early afternoon. Time for a dip. Messner led an "abandon ship" with a cannonball dive off the starboard bow.

After a brief swim, the tow line was tossed and everyone who wanted a turn held on for a different kind of a ride. My swimming suit drawstrings weren't tight enough, and as I was being dragged through the water, the suit came off. I was able to catch them at my ankles and clench tightly for the remainder of my adrenaline rush, saving myself from an embarrassing predicament. When the boat slowed, I was able to pull my trunks back on. I later told Messner about this, and he could not stop laughing.

Two years earlier, I had gone swimming at Hanauma Bay on the southeast tip of Oahu the day after Michigan beat Hawaii. As I got past the white coral reefs of Keyhole Lagoon and swam into the channel, I ran into Messner and receiver Paul Jokisch. We began stroking together, enjoying the warm saltwater on a day when it was freezing cold back home. But we came upon a metal sign, warning us to avoid dangerous currents by turning back. Messner shook his head and kept swimming out toward the Pacific Ocean, beyond the bay. And we followed, luckily avoiding any problems.

Messner was confident there, just as he was on a football field, that nothing could stop him.

I thought back to that time in the much cooler water of one of the Great Lakes after my wild ride. The pull of the tow was hard on the arms but refreshing. "Hey, is this great or what?" Messner asked.

The motor that had been turned on to speed up the tow was cut off after 10 or 15 minutes, and the swimming party was asked to re-board ship. Messner, dripping wet, made his way to the mast. He grabbed it, snarled like a pirate and shouted, "Aaargh, mateys!" Someone began singing a Jimmy Buffet song of the sea, and stories of old sailing trips and parties began flowing.

Messner was part of Captain Poleck's crew in the 1986 Port Huron to Mackinac Race, a prestigious two-day test of navigation, daring, and skill. But more often than not, sailing is a way to reach Grosse Ile for a special dinner, the Cedar Point amusement park, or Put-in-Bay.

"Put-in-Bay is a fun place," Messner said. "People are having a good time there. But some of them get carried away. There's this one boat called the Duck Boat that was banned from the island. These guys would do anything."

There was plenty of down time on the sail, and Messner took advantage of it to talk to everyone and horse around with Gillette. They roomed together off campus and became close. We also had a chance to talk some football and about closing his career on the proper note.

Messner entered the season five tackles short of the school record for tackles made behind the line of scrimmage, trailing only the 48 for minus-234 yards set by Curtis Greer, an All-American defensive tackle in 1979.

"Getting to 49 tackles [behind the line] means quite a bit to me,"

Messner said. "It's the only record I really want. To be No. 1 there would be a hell of an honor at a school like Michigan."

Messner was asked for his favorite tackle. "I don't really have one," he said. After some coaxing, the 30-yard chase to sack Northwestern quarterback Mike Greenfield was recalled.

His reaction was quite different when asked for his worst mistake. The response was immediate: "Notre Dame. My freshman year. There were two reverses. I got to the play both times and missed. I read the keys properly and just missed them." Two mistakes came to mind quicker than 44 big plays. Such is the thought pattern of a perfectionist.

For his career at Michigan, Messner shattered not only Greer's record but the career sacks record set by Robert Thompson, who had 19 from 1979–82.

Messner was named the Big Ten's Defensive Lineman of the Year in 1988 after making eight sacks and setting the school record with 26 tackles for losses. He is the hands-down most productive front-four player in school history.

His 70 tackles behind the line for 376 yards and 36 sacks remain school records through the 2012 season. A quarter-century has passed and schedules have increased from 11 games in his era to 12 games, but nobody has come close to Messner's numbers. Great players such as 2006 Lombardi Award–winner LaMarr Woodley and 2009 All-Big Ten end Brandon Graham have come up well short of Messner.

The Sporting News had Messner and Bo on the cover of its 1988 college football magazine that summer. The publication ranked the Wolverines No. 1, and Messner held his index finger high as the coach smiled widely in the photo.

"People ask me what it's like to be in Bo's doghouse," Messner said. "I tell them that I've been lucky. When I got here, Bo said, 'I have my eye on you. You get out of line and I'm going to come down on you like rain.'

"I guess that fear kept me clean. You find out that Bo knows about everything that goes on on this campus. So the best thing is to avoid situations that can get you in trouble. Bo is intimidating when you come in. But then you find yourself wandering into his office to talk about everything but football. I have to thank Bo and the people at Michigan for developing me as a man and a person."

Bo was the third father figure in Messner's life. First was his father, Max Messner, the former Detroit Lions and Pittsburgh Steelers linebacker. But his parents divorced when he was young. Then his mother, Sharon, married Pretty. Messner maintained contact with Max but was raised by Pretty in Hartland, Michigan, just north of Ann Arbor. He called them both Dad.

"It took me an hour and a half to get this guy to bed when he was little," Pretty said. "Gosh, he was something. You'd have to pin him down at bed time to sit still. He'd make you want to strangle him. All my tools disappeared in the woods with him. Then he went to school and all that changed. The teacher said, 'Mark is so well behaved.'"

Pretty rolled his eyes. Kids.

Messner owned up to the reputation. "I got into everything," he said. "Mom called me The Pistol. She would say that her big wish was that someday I had a kid just like me. I broke things in stores all the time. It was heaven for me but hell for Mom. When they took me to the beach in Florida, I wore a dog harness attached to a 20' rope."

The group laughs at the thought. "We can do that *now*," said Pretty, stressing the last word and smiling. Messner is hope for every parent with a Dennis the Menace child.

Once ashore, I made my way to Bo's office to talk to him about the menace of his defensive line.

"Messner is a great kid," Bo said. "He works hard, plays hard, and goes to school. He spends a lot of time visiting kids in hospitals. He's the kind of kid you want."

Bo watched Messner all right, just like he said he would. And Bo loved what he saw every step of the way.

Messner took out a $3,000 loan that summer. But it wasn't for a car (his was a 1980 Oldsmobile Toronado that topped 160,000 miles). He wanted to enjoy his last summer as a college kid and "lift weights like never before."

Maturity has a way of putting its own dog harness on you. Messner realized that. And so there was something more than just that summer slipping away.

His college days, days he cherished, were months from conclusion.

While Graham (Philadelphia Eagles, first round) and Pro Bowl pick Woodley (Pittsburgh Steelers, second round) were high draft picks who could not match Messner's college numbers, they thrived in the pros. Messner, considered undersized at 6'2" and 256 pounds, lasted until the sixth round in 1989 when the Los Angeles Rams drafted him. He impressed Rams coach John Robinson, the former Southern Cal coach who was close to Bo, but Messner played in only four games in his rookie season. Robinson sought for ways to use Messner, a very active "tweener" who was too small for the line and too slow to play linebacker.

But he never got a shot at developing.

"My knee injury was a dandy for my one and only football injury—career ender," Messner said. "Took out my ACL, LCL, and MCL along with my meniscus on the 26-yard line of Candlestick Park versus the 49ers in the NFC Championship Game. Last time I ever put on football gear. Bad day!"

He tore the anterior, lateral, and medial collateral ligaments in the knee, and his NFL career was over. But Messner did well with his degree in business administration and is a market vice president for Konica Minolta Solutions living in Bradenton, Florida.

The photo for his LinkedIn professional networking profile features Messner wearing a sport coat, an open-collar shirt, and a wide smile. On the wall behind him is a framed color photo of Bo on the field during a game, grinning and wearing sunglasses.

Bo signed it, "Mark, you are one of my greatest players and a true friend."

CHAPTER 9

Twenty-Four Hours to Kickoff with Mark Messner

Want to spend the 24 hours to kickoff with a Michigan All-American?

Mark Messner detailed that build-up to the frenzy of game day in Ann Arbor in a column I wrote for the *Ann Arbor News* in 1987. And here is his take on that experience, beginning with Messner's last class on Friday:

"In class, I drift off to my assignments and the game. I have to snap out of it and pay attention. Finally, it's time to leave for practice at 1:00.

"We have these special blue sweats that the travel team wears for Friday practices. We put those on with our helmets and go through a short practice. We work on the hurry-hurry, which is the two-minute offense and defense. Then all phases of the kick game are worked on.

"We have a crowd-noise drill, where we surround the quarterback and he has to make his check-offs and audibles over it. On the last play, Bo [Schembechler] plays quarterback or receiver. He scores a touchdown, and we all cheer. It's pretty funny and relieves the tension."

Bo was a no-glory offensive guard at Miami of Ohio. But as a coach, he got to score a touchdown every week.

"We watch films and have meetings and take a bus down State Street to the Campus Inn. It's total silence on the bus. Nobody says anything. Guys at the frats wave and holler and people clap as we get off the bus. But you feel stone cold, serious.

"At dinner, all you can hear is the tinkling of forks and plates.

Everybody is too busy thinking. That all changes after we eat and the film is put on. We watch a movie, something like Clint Eastwood, and hoot on each other. We relax.

"We go up to our rooms at about 10:00. My roommate is [defensive tackle] Dave Folkertsma. We take off our suits and put on shorts and T-shirts. It's time to take our team tests. After that we might listen to the radio or a little TV. The coaches check in.

"Then you try to go to sleep, but most are too nervous to do that. It's a really good feeling, though. There's no way to stray from the so-called mission. There's no girl to talk to or any phone ringing to distract you. You have no obligation to the worldly things. I lay there and try to picture how I'm going to beat my man. That way, when I get in the game, it feels as if I've already done it. You settle down, but it's still hard to sleep. The fire station is just a few blocks down, and you hear the trucks taking off all night."

The wakeup call comes at 7:00 AM.

"We put on shorts and shirts and go down to a room to get taped. Knee braces get put on at the stadium. We have a pregame meal, and it's quiet again. Then it's time for the defensive and offensive meetings.

"We get a police escort to the stadium, and the defense rides together in the second bus. It starts out like the other bus ride. You are cold and oblivious. Then you see the tailgaters clapping, and you start getting excited. We're going through red lights, and it feels like nothing can stop us.

"Everyone crowds up to the busses, and the fans are singing, 'Hail to the Victors.' It's quite a boost. You're already jacked."

But it's a brief rush and much too early. Once inside the locker room, the quiet returns.

"The only conversations you have are with trainers and coaches. They set up chalkboards to partition the room, but it's hard to hear your coach over the other coaches in the room.

"After the last details, it's time to go out. And I don't know if you can even write about what it's like in the tunnel. It's a feeling you can't explain. I try to tell the freshmen to hold on. They'll want to pee their pants.

"Then we come running out, and all you see are helmets bobbing up and down. You have to restrain yourself from jumping too high to hit the [M Club] banner at midfield. You become engulfed in the noise. You have no feeling for a bit. Again, it's hard to explain. It's something no one else can imagine.

"I pace on the sideline before the kickoff. I can't wait to get out there. But once you're out there, it's not like you might imagine. It's a lot like the movies. I can't hear the crowd, and it looks like the quarterback is moving in slow motion.

"I'm so focused that I can hear guys breathing. The only time the crowd comes back is on the sideline. I missed the whole wave thing. After that first play, all the butterflies are gone. It's like a scrimmage."

CHAPTER 10

Desmond Howard:
From Stockbridge Avenue to Greatness

The two-story, two-bedroom house on Stockbridge Avenue blended into the rest of a modest neighborhood. It was painted white and yellow with green trim, and it was tucked away on the far east side of Cleveland.

Nothing seemed special about it. But looks can be deceiving. It was the home of a Heisman Trophy winner, a tight family with successful children, and it once even doubled as a place of business. Desmond Howard's mother, Hattie Dawkins, and her husband, Floyd, still lived there with Desmond's youngest brother, Jermaine.

His parents, Hattie and J.D. Howard, made the most of the limited space before they were divorced seven years prior to Desmond winning the Heisman Trophy. Hattie ran a day-care nursery out of the den, which became Desmond's trophy room. The four boys were crammed into one bedroom. Jonathan and Chad Jones, his mother's sons from a previous marriage, shared one bunk, and Desmond and Jermaine shared another. They were as close as brothers could be—literally and figuratively.

Jonathan, then 25, was an Air Force sergeant who served as a flight mechanic in the Persian Gulf War. Chad, then 24, was a plumber in Cleveland. Jermaine, then 17, was an outstanding student and track-and-field runner at Villa Angela-St. Joseph High. And then there was Desmond—the little brother's hero and everybody's joy, the most famous receiver Michigan has ever produced.

His mother had never seen a picture of the famous trophy her son won until that fall of 1991. When her son struck the Heisman pose after his 93-yard punt return for a touchdown against Ohio State, she didn't realize he was imitating the straight-arming pose of the most famous trophy in college sports.

"I just thought Desmond was clowning around," Hattie said. "But I knew all about what the Heisman meant. Still, whenever I asked about it or getting a dress and tuxedos for the banquet, Desmond ignored me. He never ignores me.

"But the first thing he said after the Ohio State game was, 'Now, what was that you were saying about a dress and tuxedo?' And he was laughing. He had kept all the pressure inside himself, but then he was a volcano erupting. He had weathered the storm and the pressure."

And so he struck the pose, grinning from ear to ear, in what has become the most replayed moment in Michigan football history.

"We didn't like the individual part of him doing that," Wolverines head coach Gary Moeller told me. "We want Michigan players to celebrate as a team—go congratulate the guys who did the blocking. I talked to Desmond about it and said, 'But with how bad you wanted to beat them, we have to go along with it.' Still, I'd rather have guys act like Barry Sanders and just flip the ball to the official. Act like you've been there 100 times."

Desmond scored 37 touchdowns at Michigan and just happened to put an exclamation point on that last one.

He was nicknamed "Magic" as a young basketball player and never set out to win the award for the nation's most outstanding college football player. All he ever wanted to do was play the game he loved and win, and nothing could stop him from that.

"If Desmond had two broken legs," his mother said, "he would find a way to climb to the mountaintop."

The view from "Magic" Mountain was sweet, indeed, but the road there was steep.

His parents spent a Sunday afternoon driving around Cleveland with me, retracing Desmond's athletic trail. J.D. recalled the laps run on the muddy St. Tim's field. He remembered how practices ran long and into the dark at St. Joe's with cold winds whipping off Lake Erie.

Getting to practice was a chore in itself. Desmond rode his bike with the banana seat two miles each way down some mean streets to practice each night with St. Tim's, a CYO team for eighth- and ninth-graders.

"I could have just walked down the street and played with another team," Desmond said. "But I wanted to play for the best, and St. Tim's was the Michigan of the peewee leagues."

Choosing a challenge over convenience continued in high school. John F. Kennedy High was a short walk from his home, but he rode two hours each morning on a series of buses to reach St. Joe, a Catholic prep school that merged with a Catholic girls school not long after he graduated in 1988.

Desmond always took the long road, the one less traveled. And as poet Robert Frost once wrote, that made all the difference. "I learned the value of sacrifice," Desmond said. "I had to cut loose friends to go to St. Joe's and wake up at 5:30 AM. You have to sacrifice to be the best and have a plan."

His parents saw to that.

J.D. said, "When he was three months old, Hattie saw this show on *Donahue* about babies swimming because it was so much like the womb. We took him to the YMCA, where I worked part-time, and he was swimming at three months. That built up his muscles and brought about his sense of acrobatics.

"We fed the boy goat's milk and guinea meat—that's meat from a young chicken—and eating the right things was important to his development."

Hattie earned a college degree as a dietary technician and was a field representative for the Ohio Hunger Task Force. She evaluated day-care menus and staged nutritional workshops. Her kids ate sound meals, but eating wasn't a rigid regimen. "I ate some Big Macs," Desmond said.

J.D. was active in his son's athletic development but not overbearing. "His dad was always at practices," said Ron Bayduke, the offensive coordinator at St. Joseph. "We would work on our two-minute offense, and I would look up at Mr. Howard in the bleachers. He would be laughing and give a thumbs up or thumbs down.

"St. Joe was a unique family operation, and the Howards fit right in."

Desmond was appreciative that his parents, though no longer married, came together so often for him because of football. They openly praised one another for the job each did with him.

"Coming from a family that breaks up does not dictate that you will become a juvenile delinquent," Desmond said. "J.D. and my mother both stressed that you must take responsibility for yourself."

And they took responsibility for motivating their children. Desmond was sent on class trips to France and Sweden, and if that meant driving a car with more than 100,000 miles on it, well, it was worth it. Sacrifice was a two-way street.

"I owe everything to both of them," Desmond said. "I get my humanitarian qualities from my mom. My love of children came from working with her day-care kids. The competitiveness comes from my father. J.D. is an extremist—a competitor who believes you finish what you start."

J.D. lights up a room when he enters; he makes others smile more quickly than even his son can. But he also has a fire inside. "I always tell Desmond to get that education because I did not get much," J.D. said. "I spent a four-year apprenticeship at the Max Hayes Trade School in Cleveland as a tool-and-die maker. I repair machines for Osborn Manufacturing in Cleveland and do okay.

"I always wished I had gone to college, though."

Desmond got his degree from Michigan that coming May, graduating in less than four years. He left for the NFL with a year of eligibility remaining, having nothing left to prove as a college player with a degree in hand.

And while touring Cleveland with his parents just days before he won the Heisman, his father made a surprising proposal. J.D. asked if I would consider being his son's agent because they trusted me. I never spoke to Desmond about that, and I declined pretty quickly while thanking J.D. for a very flattering thought. I would've needed to find a lawyer familiar with player contracts and walk away from journalism—but I wanted to continue doing what I loved.

Desmond was the fourth overall pick in the first round by the Washington Redskins that April, and he was a great kick returner but a nondescript receiver during 11 pro seasons. However, he was named MVP of Super Bowl XXXI for sparking the Green Bay Packers' victory over the New England Patriots by returning a kickoff 99 yards for a touchdown and tying a Super Bowl record with 244 return yards.

He became a popular announcer on ESPN's *College GameDay* after retiring as a player.

Desmond's parents kept him motivated academically and athletically, and his well-roundedness allowed him to succeed as a broadcaster because he related so well to a wide-range of personalities. J.D. and Hattie made sure to provide stiff challenges that channeled their son's energy and kept him off the streets.

"The child almost never slept," Hattie said. "He would take a nap for 15 minutes and be refreshed! You've heard of the terrible twos? Well, he was the terrible ones right on up.

"He used to pull everything off the shelves out of boredom. So we got him this pinball game in the basement, and it was jumping all day."

Howard always got his work done first at Gracemount Elementary and became a fidgety disturbance waiting for the rest to catch up. That was remedied by putting him in enrichment courses and placing him in an honors program.

They learned not to question his ambition, but his size always caused doubts.

Desmond Kevin Howard was a big baby—9 lbs., 14 oz. at birth—but he wasn't large for long. At 5'9", 176 lbs., he was the smallest player on the Michigan roster in 1991. But he became the biggest player on campus since 1940 Heisman Trophy winner Tom Harmon.

Looks can be deceiving.

Howard's size was first tested at Gracemount. He played there with his older brothers and their friends on a 30-yard-long patch of grass. The out-of-bounds markers were the school wall and a sidewalk, and iron bars two feet off the ground surrounded the field.

It was part obstacle course, part football field.

"Desmond scored more touchdowns than all the big guys," Jermaine said, "and they would say, 'We're gonna get you, Dez!'"

One day they tried to take a touchdown away from Desmond, and he punched Chad in the mouth before running. He streaked down 161st Street for three blocks to Stockbridge and made a quick right to his front steps before racing through the door.

"We all chased him, but nobody could catch him," Jonathan said. "And that's why that boy got so fast; he had to run away from us and the concrete sideline."

Desmond laughed and said, "Hey, give me a head start and it's over."

Having speed is one thing. Having direction is an entirely different thing, and J.D. made sure his sons had that, too. J.D. used to point to the thugs on street corners and tell his sons, "That's their education right there, learning to sell drugs. And all they will ever get for it is a fancy car. You will never be there, and years from now they will still be right there."

When Desmond picked up on that wisdom or any other valuable point, J.D. would smile and say, "You're right! You're exactly right!"

Positive reinforcement went a long way.

When Desmond returned home from college, everyone pointed at him. The neighbors would tell their children, "Look at Desmond Howard. Look at what you could become.'"

Young fans and old friends rang the doorbell to pose with Desmond and ask for autographs when word spread or neighbors noticed he was home. He smiled and made a fuss over each one.

"We went to the car wash," Hattie said, "and I looked at him and said, 'Desmond, aren't you tired of this?' And he said, 'No, Mom. I'm having the time of my life.'"

CHAPTER 11

Desmond Howard:
David Letterman and the Heisman Trophy Weekend

When Desmond Howard received the formal invitation from the Downtown Athletic Club of New York as a finalist for the 1991 Heisman Trophy, I had one simple question for him: "Who do you like better, Leno or Letterman?"

Desmond immediately answered, "Letterman, for sure. I watch the guy almost every night—cracks me up."

I then asked Desmond if he wanted to see *Late Show with David Letterman* the night before the December 14 Heisman presentation.

"Absolutely, man," he said. "Can you get tickets?"

I told Desmond that I could, and he was excited about it.

The year before, while covering the NCAA Basketball Tournament, I wanted to write about Letterman's infatuation with his alma mater, Ball State, which had advanced to the Sweet 16. The unheralded Cardinals had beaten Oregon State and Louisville to become Cinderellas, and Letterman took joy in celebrating them in his nightly monologues.

So I got in touch with his office at NBC-TV and asked for an interview. One of Letterman's assistants told me, "Dave doesn't want to do a phone interview but likes your story idea. He asked that you fax me three questions, and I'll fax back his answers to you."

That worked for me.

Letterman replied with some funny lines (no surprise there) for a piece before Ball State played UNLV and lost by just two points. One of his assistants called after I faxed the article to Letterman and said he liked the story. "Call me anytime you are in town, and we'll get you some tickets," she added.

So I got tickets for the two of us and Wolverines sports information director Bruce Madej for the December 13 show. And after all the Friday interviews and obligations, we put on our coats and walked outside to hail a cab. One of the Heisman reps spotted Desmond and asked if we needed a limousine ride anywhere. This is how you get treated when you are with the Heisman Trophy favorite.

We headed toward midtown in luxury and arrived outside NBC Studios early for the show. So we wandered around and took in the Rockefeller Center Christmas Tree, a towering Norway pine more than 70' tall and decorated with an elaborate chain of lights. There were even sidewalk vendors roasting chestnuts on an open fire. Manhattan at Christmas is something to behold and cherish.

Once inside the studio at 30 Rockefeller Plaza, we went to the reception desk and waited. *Free Press* photographer Julian Gonzalez, who was chronicling Desmond's coronation weekend with me, met us there. We were soon escorted to Studio 6B, the same studio where *Late Night with Jimmy Fallon* is now taped and where *The Tonight Show* with both Johnny Carson and Jack Paar was taped.

Letterman's producer, Robert Morton, told us that he wanted us to sit front row and center for the show and be introduced after his monologue. Actually, he was only concerned about Desmond being there but was going to give us the royal treatment, too. This was great. I was a huge fan of the show and Letterman, and I would fantasize about writing a best-seller and getting invited as a guest to discuss my prose with the current king of late night.

"Well," Desmond said, "I am flattered by this. Don't take this the wrong way, but I would rather just sit in the green room and watch the show from there with the guests."

What?

I asked Desmond if he had, well, lost his mind.

"I just don't want to jinx winning the award by doing this," he told me in all sincerity.

I explained to him that he gets plenty of shots at network television, but this brief "brush with greatness" was my only shot. Besides, it was widely agreed that Desmond was going to be a landslide winner. It is also impossible to jinx winning an award that has already had the vote completed and tallied.

"C'mon, Dez, have a heart," I said.

"Nope," he answered, "just can't jinx it."

And then Desmond dropped his head back and laughed that infectious, high-pitched laugh of his. And I knew there was no talking him out of this.

Wide receiver Desmond Howard poses with the Heisman Trophy at New York's Downtown Athletic Club on December 14, 1991. (AP Photo/Mark Lennihan)

The green room it was.

Virtually every entertainment star of the last 60 years had sat in there, waiting for Jack, Johnny, Dave, or Jimmy to call them into the chair next to their desk. Okay, so we got Jack Hanna and his zoo animals and Los Lobos, which had performed on the *La Bamba* soundtrack the year before. But they were pretty cool guys, and we got to pet an aardvark or some such exotic animal.

We had hoped to spend a few minutes with Letterman after the show, but he had something going on. Still, Morton said he was sorry about that and was glad to have us at the show.

Desmond and I watched the whole show on a big monitor screen, and Letterman was on his game. I can't recall a single joke from the monologue or a barb he hurled at Hanna, who was wearing that crazy safari hat. But I can remember how loudly we laughed. Oh, we just howled.

The show was taped just before the dinner hour in order to have the proper amount of time to set it up on satellite for the time slot at 12:35 AM. So that night I curled up in my bed at the Downtown Athletic Club and watched the show again. And since there is no ceiling to the green room, which is adjacent to the stage and set, I could hear Desmond cackling and me laughing way too loud.

And I laughed some more.

Meeting Tom Brokaw after the show was anything but a rush. Word had spread that Desmond was in Rockefeller Center, and the *NBC Nightly News* anchor requested his presence in his office. We were on the elevator and down the hall to Brokaw's sprawling office.

Desmond told Brokaw, "You're smooth, like Brent Musburger." They laughed and Brokaw complimented him for his abilities and desires to help various charities once he turned pro—an announcement that would come after the Rose Bowl.

Brokaw absolutely gushed over Desmond but acted as if the rest of us shouldn't have been allowed in. He gave us dead-fish handshakes and quickly looked away to ask questions of Desmond. I wanted to say, "A frown and a smile take the same amount of time." But I resisted, and we all left after a short time.

However, the night was young, and there was more fun in store. Madej invited me to join him at a special dinner for sports information directors, the Heisman finalists, and their immediate families. So I got to meet and eat with the Howards; BYU quarterback Ty Detmer, who had won the 1990 Heisman; and University of Washington defensive tackle Steve Emtman, who would be chasing Desmond around the Rose Bowl in less than three weeks. Florida State quarterback Casey Weldon, the other finalist, didn't arrive until Saturday because he was receiving the Johnny Unitas Golden Arm Trophy that night in Louisville, Kentucky.

The finalists present were handed white footballs bearing the Heisman stamp and were encouraged to get autographs from past Heisman winners in the dining room at the Jack Mowbray Grill.

"You might as well autograph mine right now," Emtman told Desmond, reaching across the appetizers to hand over the football.

Everyone laughed, and the obvious was foreshadowed.

Desmond moved to the corner table with Detmer to get the autograph of the first of 56 previous winners, the University of Chicago's Jay Berwanger, who had a truly unique game confrontation with another outstanding Michigan gridder.

Berwanger, according to the *University of Chicago Chronicle*, was the only Heisman recipient who was ever tackled by a future President—Gerald Ford, during a 1934 game between Chicago and Michigan. "When I tackled Jay in the second quarter, I ended up with a bloody cut [beneath the left eye] and I still have the scar to prove it," Ford recalled in the publication.

However, Berwanger, who died in 2002 at the age of 88, took it easy on Desmond and just signed the ball.

You could feel the history of Heismans past at the Downtown Athletic Club, housed in a 35-story art deco–style building that was completed in 1930. From 1935 through 2000, from initial recipient Berwanger through Florida State quarterback Chris Weinke, the Heisman was presented there. It was built just off the Hudson River and less than a half mile south of the World Trade Center.

When the terrorists overtook the planes that downed the World Trade Center on September 11, 2001, the DAC was fortunate to avoid destruction. But it was in a "frozen zone" and closed, never to reopen as the DAC, which filed for bankruptcy one year later. It opened in 2005 as the Downtown Club Condominium and continues as a residence near the Wall Street district.

The Heisman would move around town and be presented at other locations in the years after that, and that quaint feeling of the award was never quite the same. But I can still recall catching a limo for the Letterman show outside the lobby at 20 West St. and the excitement of that chilly night in Manhattan.

Hanging with the toast of the town definitely has its advantages.

CHAPTER 12

Forty Hours Recruiting with Lloyd Carr

Lloyd Carr was driving down I–94 in Chicago with a cup of coffee in his right hand and a phone in his left hand, which was pressed to his ear. He was steering with his knees and talking to his secretary about changing travel plans on a recruiting trip that knew no end. It was a free-form method of travel, where the next flight or drive was to wherever he was needed to close a deal and get a commitment from a high school football star.

National letter-of-intent signing day was approaching, and there was a Big Ten championship team to build.

I was seated next to him in a rental car, wondering who was insuring this crazy driver, when Carr looked at me and said, "Hey Steve, hand me a pen so I can write this down."

I laughed and said I was not handing him anything more because he was already out of hands. And I offered to write down the phone number he was taking over the phone, saving us from a sure pileup on the Dan Ryan Expressway.

Carr agreed to let me fly, drive, and run through the Midwest with him so I could write about the essence of recruiting for the *Detroit Free Press*. Jerome Bettis was the big target for Carr that winter, and Bettis was constantly on Carr's mind during our travels.

Photographer Al Kamuda accompanied us and took some great shots—including one that was not published but hangs in Carr's den. It is of Carr, back to the photographer, using the urinal in an Illinois high school rest room. Lloyd laughed hard when Al gave it to him, framed no less, and it tied into his ability to laugh at himself and roll with the punches. Carr was hard to catch off-guard, and that tied into his success as a coach.

That ability to deal with the unexpected was so evident on those recruiting trips.

Head coach Gary Moeller threw in an unscheduled visit to linebacker Pete Bercich at Providence Catholic High outside of Joliet, Illinois, and doing so nearly made us miss our flight out of Midway Airport on the outskirts of Chicago.

I checked my watch as we neared Midway and figured there was no way we were going to make the flight leaving in less than a half hour. And we still had a rental car to return. But Carr knew what he was doing.

"We're parking this car right here at the curb outside the entrance," Carr said. "I'll call my secretary and have her take care of the check-in."

We made the flight by a couple minutes.

The pace was maddening. We would leave hotels at 7:00 AM and check into another one in some other state at 11:00 PM. It was exhausting going from school to school and home to home. But Carr always appeared fresh, wide-eyed, and ready to go. I was dragging at times. But then, Carr drank all that coffee.

And he was that way day after day. Carr had an ability to make each player feel as if he was the only one Carr was recruiting. What neither of us knew during this undertaking was that we were breaking a little-known NCAA rule that deemed it to be an unfair advantage for reporters to accompany coaches on recruiting trips. Bo Schembechler, who had just retired as coach and stayed on as the athletic director, had approved my request for this one-of-a-kind journalistic voyage. And when he discovered, after the trip, that it was a violation, Bo turned in the details to the NCAA as a form of self-reporting.

Bo also called and asked that the *Free Press* not run the feature. I explained that it was a horse-out-of-the-barn matter. The violation had occurred whether the story ran or not. However, I called *Free Press* sports editor Dave Robinson, the man who hired me, and put the decision in his hands. Robinson said the story would run. Bo actually handled this decision quite well, to my surprise. And the penalty that came down for this minor infraction was taking Carr and linebackers coach Jim Herrmann, who spent a good deal of time with us one day, from going on the road the first two days of recruiting that next spring.

Carr visited 13 high school players on our 40-hour journey together, and each player was quite different. So were the settings in which we met them. But Carr's methods varied little from place to place and player to player. At times he was Willie Loman, the insistent traveling salesman with a pitch. At others he was Jimmy Stewart—the description given by recruit Greg McThomas' mother—a comforting conversationalist. Carr could read the moment and sense whether it was time to close or to keep building the relationship.

Here is what it was like to experience the essence of recruiting the nation's top players:

Wednesday, January 17, 8:06 AM: It is foggy, rainy, and miserable—a day that prompts long faces. Unless you are the football coach and recruits are waiting.

"Are you fired up?" Carr asked. "You better be because you're going recruiting."

Carr backed out of a driveway in Ann Arbor, headed for Metro Airport and a flight to Green Bay. Jim Flanigan, the *Detroit Free Press'* defensive player of the year in the Midwest, lives just north of town in the little hamlet of Brussels.

The rush-hour traffic on I–94 offers no major road blocks and, after parking in the airport lot, he is quickly in the terminal.

"If Mo were with us, we'd be running now," Carr said, referring to head coach Gary Moeller. "Mo is never late and never early. He always just cuts it to the bone. Me, I like to leave a few minutes for a cup of coffee and my morning newspaper."

Moeller had replaced Bo one month earlier and was putting together his first class as head coach. If that transition had occurred in the era Brady Hoke is coaching in, the majority of the class would have been committed in December. But in that era, you could count the commitments at the end of the regular season on one hand.

Carr buys apple turnovers and coffee and boards at the last minute. The pilot announces, "Your flight is canceled. The visibility in Green Bay is 1/16th of a mile. Please return to the ticket counter." Carr forces a smile and says, "This is the first flight I've had canceled in five years, but there's nothing more frustrating. Well, welcome to recruiting. Now we'll have to juggle things. Aaahrgh!"

He calls Flanigan to arrange a later meeting but is told not to come. Flanigan has picked Notre Dame. "If we got on that plane," Carr said, "he probably would've said the same thing to me. But you never know."

Flanigan was an All-America selection for the Fighting Irish in 1993, anchored the defensive line of the Chicago Bears for several years and was named the Walter Payton NFL Man of the Year in 2001.

12:35 PM: Carr arranges for a later flight to Milwaukee, and the extra time allows a brief swing through Detroit. All the coaches have different geographical areas of concentration, and Carr's are Wisconsin and metropolitan Detroit.

Carr does not want to use one of six allowed visits with Harper Woods Bishop Gallagher tailback Jesse Johnson on this day, but Carr does check in with Johnson's coach, George Sahadi. But I suspect the real reason is to have lunch with a man who knows how to eat.

"Here, have some spinach pie and kibbeh I got from a Lebanese place on Outer Drive," says Sahadi, unwrapping the food in tin foil.

"George," Carr says, "you're the best." They have known each other since Carr began coaching at Detroit Nativity in 1968. Stories of the old times are rolling as Michigan State defensive coordinator Norm Parker enters.

"Norm, this is for you," says Carr, pointing to the few remaining scraps of food. They all laugh, and Carr, placing his arm on Parker's shoulder, says, "Norm, we all know your colors are green and white. But is it for Michigan State or the New York Jets?"

Parker rolls his eyes, laughs, and makes a crack about Carr's golf game. He never answers the Jets question but isn't expected to. The next week, MSU coach George Perles nearly left for that NFL team.

Next stop is Detroit King, where free safety Deon Johnson is waiting. King coach Jim Reynolds meets Carr in the gym and introduces him to Johnson.

"Lloyd, his parents paid you a big compliment," Reynolds says. "They said you are the only one not bad-mouthing other schools. They say you just talked up Michigan."

Johnson & Johnson—Jesse and Deon—will pick Michigan. Deon became a starting cornerback, and Jesse had four 100-yard rushing games while managing to contribute despite the tailback spot being loaded in his years with Tyrone Wheatley and Ricky Powers ahead of him.

3:45 PM: The plane is pulling away from the gate at Metro, bound for Milwaukee. Carr is scheduled to visit Racine Park High tailback Brent Moss and McThomas, an outside linebacker from Milwaukee Marquette. Carr falls asleep but is jolted as the jet surges into the clouds. "I have to tell you I hate flying," he says. "How's that for a guy in my business?"

5:26 PM: Carr rents a car, pulls out of the airport and onto the highway for Racine. The phone, his connection to recruits and headquarters in Ann Arbor, is placed on the dashboard.

"Lynn," says Carr, addressing football secretary Lynn Koch, "give me some good news! ...okay then, give me Bo...Bo, no, we didn't get Flanigan. He said he loved Michigan and everything but always wanted to go to Notre Dame. Bo, it broke my heart. But McThomas had a great visit with us last weekend, and I think we have a legitimate shot at him. He is as blessed physically as any kid I've seen. We've got to get him."

Bo, the school's athletic director until March 1, gets updates on football developments. This is the last class he will reach out and touch.

6:00 PM: After stopping twice to ask for directions and nearly running over a neighborhood poodle, Carr pulls into the driveway in middle-class Racine. The two car license plates there have MOSS 1 and MOSS 2.

No need to check the address.

Moss is scheduled to visit Ann Arbor on February 2, and Carr is pleased to learn that his parents will accompany him. They discuss academics in the living room, and Carr issues his pitch.

"It's been the Bo & Mo show for 18 of the last 21 years at Michigan," he said. "Gary knows the Michigan tradition; we anticipate no changes. We went to January 1 bowl games eight times in the 1980s. The Center of Champions for football will be ready in August and is second to none.

"I could tell you, 'You're our No. 1 back.' But if we get someone better, you're No. 2. That's because what happens on the field is up to you. We instill team and family, and we don't give cars, clothes, or anything illegal. Ours is not a fragmented team full of jealousy. Coach [Phil] Dobbs has told me you're unselfish and can appreciate that."

Carr stops and gives the family and opportunity to enter the conversation, but instead there is an awkward silence.

"Uh, Brent, what are your goals?" Carr asks. "What do you want in a school?"

"I want a weight room that I can use at any time," Moss said. "I want to win the Heisman Trophy."

Carr collects himself, somehow manages not to smile, and says, "Brent, those are high aspirations.... Now look at where the Heisman winners come from—established programs."

Carr does not mention that Michigan has not had a Heisman winner since Tom Harmon in 1940. But, unbeknownst to anyone, the 1991 Heisman winner was already on campus in the person of Desmond Howard. And the 1997 Heisman would go to Wolverines cornerback

Charles Woodson.

"Tony Boles had a tremendous chance of winning it for us next year," Carr continued, "but he had an unfortunate injury. But no matter how great you are, you are not going to win the Heisman without a line knocking guys out of the way for you."

Moss nervously rubs his knee and adjusts his baseball cap. The Tracy Chapman video on the TV catches his eye, even though the sound is off. Carr isn't connecting. After an hour, Carr leaves with the assurance that the family will visit. Moss cancels the next week and commits to Wisconsin.

Michigan ends up with three tailbacks rated as high or higher than Moss, including the Midwest's top player, Ricky Powers of Akron (Ohio) Buchtel.

Moss was 5'9" and, while talented, was not even the best back in the Midwest. That season, Bettis, Powers, and Robert Smith were the best running backs in an absolutely loaded class. It was widely debated which was better. Moss was below their caliber, and yet he didn't flinch in saying he wanted to win the Heisman.

All four of those backs would have varying degrees of success in college, but Bettis and Smith would become first-round picks in the NFL. Powers and Moss would get a cup of coffee in the league.

Moss was academically ineligible as a freshman at Wisconsin but was both the Big Ten's offensive player of the year in 1993 after rushing for 1,479 yards and the 1994 Rose Bowl MVP with 158 yards and two touchdowns in a win over UCLA. However, a crack cocaine arrest in 1994 ended his hopes of breaking Wisconsin's career rushing record. Moss was suspended that November with 3,428 yards—281 shy of Billy Marek's mark.

Moss never finished in the Top 10 in Heisman voting.

7:45 PM: Heading to Milwaukee, Carr dials the phone and waits for an answer.

"Hello, Emily Carr. Now don't you be mad at me for beating you in chess. I love you.... Put Jason on, please. Jason, what's going on? Have you started baseball practice? Hey, play your sister in chess, and I'll play the winner. Okay? I love you."

He calls a list of recruits to say hello, but nothing tops the smile on his face after talking with his children. The time coaches spend away from their families is something fans never fully realize. They love their jobs, but the trade-off is having so little time away from those jobs. However, Jason Carr did get to spend some of those long hours around his father when he served as a backup quarterback for the Wolverines from 1992–95.

9:00 PM: After checking in at a Milwaukee Marriott, Carr heads to Giuseppi's for dinner. He calls Detroit (Michigan) Mackenzie fullback Jerome Bettis ("Jerome Bettis, you're No. 1 in my heart.") and still can't reach McThomas to confirm the next morning's meeting.

Nearing the completion of a plate of clams and linguine in red sauce, Carr leaves to find a pay phone. McThomas is home, and the rendezvous is set.

"I can relax now," Carr says. "Whew! What a day."

It is 10:30.

Thursday, January 18, 7:30 AM: It's off to Marquette High, an all-boys Catholic school. Carr meets McThomas and Coach Dick Basham in a counselor's room. McThomas is wearing a Michigan hat. "I like that," Carr says.

They engage in small talk, and the atmosphere is quite different than it was at the Moss home. The selling takes place almost as an afterthought.

"Just like here, the people in our business school will care about you, Tim," says Carr, confusing him with Tim Williams, the Michigan outside linebacker from the same high school.

Carr corrects himself and smiles. McThomas isn't offended, but the slip could have cost points with another player.

McThomas recalls a visit to Ann Arbor. "Tim introduced me to everybody," he says. "It was important having him there. I did not know the business school was that good. I saw a bulletin board with 300 companies recruiting from it."

Carr is beaming.

"We hope to have you, Greg," he says. "You'll have an opportunity to play early, and on a great team."

McThomas had committed to Notre Dame but changed his mind and selected Michigan. It was considered a major coup at the time, but McThomas never made an impact for the Wolverines.

9:30 AM: Carr eats what will be his only meal of the day at Heinemann's, a breakfast place he says he never misses, and hits the highway for Chicago Heights (Illinois) Bloom, where recruits Marcus Walker and Bryant Young attend.

Michigan assistant coach Les Miles (the future LSU head coach) recruits Illinois and wants Carr to visit them with him. This is cross-recruiting, when a coordinator touches base with players he will coach. That is why Miles also asked Carr to schedule time with New Lenox (Illinois) Providence linebacker Bercich, who was trying to pick a fifth school to visit.

"I think at this point—if you have to try to convince them just to visit—you're whistling Dixie," Carr says. He agreed to see him anyway.

All goes well with Young and Walker. It is a casual meeting with plenty of joking and back-slapping. The coaches' conversation drifts away from the players for an instant before Carr meets alone with Walker.

"For the first time since this started, Marcus was not my center of attention," Miles says. "I wondered what he thought about that."

Paranoia is rampant among recruiters, but Walker, brother of Wolverines starting tight end Derrick Walker, is a lock. Young picked Notre Dame.

Walker had two good years as an inside linebacker and started in 1992. Young became an All-American defensive lineman and a first-round pick by the San Francisco 49ers, for whom he helped win a Super Bowl and played in four Pro Bowls.

2:57 PM: Carr spends a frustrating half hour with Bercich, who is friendly but nervous and constantly chomping gum. Bercich admits to being confused, ticks off Carr by pointing to their poor bowl record (5–5 over the last 10 years), and becomes a waste of time.

Carr is driving like a maniac in an attempt to make a 4:00 PM flight at Midway. He calls recruiting coordinator Bob Chmiel, a Chicago native, for shortcuts.

"Bob, Miles told me this was 30 minutes to the airport, and it's an hour," Carr says. "It's going to be a miracle if we make this, and now I'm behind a danged garbage truck. Geez!"

3:46 PM: He blows into Midway and barely makes the flight. Carr naps and reads papers on the plane. He walks out of Metro at 6:15 and barely makes the Ohio State basketball game at Crisler Arena, where recruits are present as school guests.

The rush was for naught. Bercich never visits and picks Notre Dame where he is a starting linebacker before playing six years as a backup for the Minnesota Vikings.

Wednesday, January 24, 9:00 AM: After visiting Birmingham Brother Rice coach Al Fracassa and top players Gannon Dudlar and Steve Morrison—both of whom will pick Michigan and start together in the 1993 Rose Bowl win over Washington—Carr and assistant coach Herrmann drive to the nearby Embers Deli & Restaurant.

"Where is Gannon going?" asks waitress Jan "The Crusher" Jadu.

"Where do you think?" Carr asks.

"Stanford or Michigan," she says. "Any place but Notre Dame. Yecch, the thought of that!"

Everyone laughs, and Iowa State coach Jim Walden and assistant Norm Andersen enter. They have also been recruiting at Rice. The coaches joke about who drinks more coffee and admit they lose count. "I drink 30 gallons a day," Walden says. "But it doesn't matter if it's decaffeinated or not. I can't sleep anyway."

Morrison, an All-Big Ten first-team pick and co-captain in 1994, ranked eighth in school history with 360 tackles after his final season.

12:30 PM: Carr is cruising down Lakeshore Drive, past the mansions on prime waterfront property in Grosse Pointe Shores. It is only a half-hour drive, but it seems like a million miles from the inner-city neighborhood around Detroit Mackenzie, his previous stop. Carr had greeted Stags receiver Walter Smith, an early Michigan commitment, and was distraught over missing Bettis, who was home with the flu.

"I'm only allowed one visit there a week," Carr says. "This is make-it-or-break-it time, and that was important."

Carr pulls into Grosse Pointe North to congratulate outside linebacker Charlie Stumb, a recent commitment, at Coach Frank Sumbera's auto shop.

Stumb offers Carr an advance autobiography Stumb wrote in fifth grade: "Let's talk about my future right now. I am 18 years old in my first year of college. I go to U-M. I love it here. I am the best pass coverer."

Stumb, however, never letters for the Wolverines.

4:30 PM: After a late and long lunch at Penna's in Warren, Carr drives back to Ann Arbor and calls Bettis. He gets an answering machine, which has a rap song recorded by Bettis' mother, Gladys: "Leave your name…state your claim…because you don't have long."

Bettis decides to go elsewhere. His mother's new recording could be, "Leave your name…state your claim…Jerome is going to Notre Dame."

And that was how my recruiting voyage with Carr came to a close. How odd it was that Carr also was being courted by the Fighting Irish at the very same time.

We were driving outside Milwaukee one night when Carr received a phone call from a head coach at another college. It didn't take me long to realize that this other coach was offering Carr a job. And it soon became clear that it was Notre Dame coach Lou Holtz.

Holtz had just lost defensive coordinator Barry Alvarez, who became the head coach at the University of Wisconsin and would sign Moss and build the Badgers into one of the top programs in the Big Ten.

So the bottom line was that it was a lateral move being proposed. Or was it?

After speaking with Holtz for about 10 minutes, Carr hung up and took a deep breath. He looked at me, and the quiet hum of the car motor on a lonely road at night was the only sound for a few seconds. Then Carr smiled and said, "Well, I guess you know what's going on here." He chuckled, and that broke the tension. I joined in the nervous laughter.

Carr proceeded to sort out this awkward situation. I'd just had a great story fall into my lap, and Carr knew that. He noted that this situation would blow up in his face if I wrote about it at that time. He asked for me to keep it under my hat for a short time period with the promise that I would get the story first when the time was right.

And I knew that would be the case. So I agreed to honor what should have been a private moment had he not allowed me to be there with him. I asked what would make him consider going from one powerhouse program and coach to another powerhouse program and coach, realizing that money was likely the reason. But there was more to it than that. Holtz proposed the possibility of his next defensive coordinator having a possible shot at succeeding him when that time came.

Carr soon called Bo. They worked things out and after some thought Carr told Holtz he was very thankful but very happy at Michigan with his good friend Moeller becoming the new head coach. And I got my story first.

There was no way I was going to blow the cover of a coach who was a great source with that kind of guarantee. And there was no way I was going to do anything but trust one of the most honorable people I've met in athletics.

I have known Carr longer than anyone else connected to Michigan's football program. I was the sports editor at the *Eastern Echo*, the student newspaper at Eastern Michigan University, when Hurons head coach Ed

Chlebek hired Carr as his defensive backs coach. And during that first season when Carr was at EMU in 1976, I also began covering Hurons athletics as a part-time writer for the *Ann Arbor News*.

We had a great relationship from the start. And after the 1977 season, when Chlebek's turnaround at EMU earned him the Boston College head coaching job, Carr opted to go to the University of Illinois as an assistant to head coach Moeller in what was the beginning of their long working relationship and close friendship.

The Eastern Michigan players, nearly every one of those returning, signed a petition asking Carr to leave Illinois weeks into that new job to become the EMU head coach. Carr declined, saying he wanted to follow through on the new commitment he had made. That process made me realize just how well respected Carr was by the players he coached and how a commitment was something he always respected.

Holtz hired Gary Darnell as his assistant head coach and defensive coordinator—titles that could have been Carr's. But before Holtz left Notre Dame following the 1996 season, Darnell left for a similar position at the University of Texas in 1992.

When Holtz departed, his defensive coordinator, Bob Davie, did succeed him. Ironically, Davie hired away the Michigan defensive coordinator at that time, Greg Mattison, to be his defensive coordinator for the Fighting Irish. Mattison had been the defensive line coach at Texas A&M when Davie was the defensive coordinator, and Mattison also got a hefty raise and other perks to make the move that Carr did not. And in doing so, Mattison parted ways with Carr on the eve of a national championship season.

But Mattison returned to the Wolverines to help head coach Brady Hoke revive the program with a Sugar Bowl victory after the 2011 season.

It turns out that the coaches are recruited as much as the players.

CHAPTER 13

Gary Moeller:
Just Like a Good Neighbor

Gary Moeller used to live on Maywood Avenue in Ann Arbor. I had no idea that he did until we moved into a house in the same neighborhood and by chance I picked out a jogging route that took me down Maywood and onto Stadium Boulevard en route to either Almendinger Park or Michigan Stadium.

One hot summer day I was huffing and puffing my way down Maywood when a familiar face came into view in the front yard of this two-story brick house that I always thought looked a bit like a castle. It was Moeller, and he waved me over.

He chuckled about us being neighbors, asked how many miles I was going, and said I better get back on the run. "You don't want to tighten up," Moeller said. "But good seeing you."

Over the years I would see his wife, Ann, much more than her husband. She would be out tending to her flowers and was such a vibrant and friendly person. Ann's brother, Joe Morrison, the former New York Giants star nicknamed "Old Dependable," ended up coaching against his brother-in-law, Gary, and nephew, U-M linebacker Andy Moeller, in 1985 as the head coach at the University of South Carolina. Moeller and the Morrisons hailed from Lima, Ohio, where the passion for football is great.

I was riding bikes with my sons past their house one day, and Gary invited us in to talk and share glasses of ice-cold lemonade that Ann had on the kitchen counter. He made a fuss over my boys, showed them some football mementoes, and told a few stories.

A reporter and a football coach can be good neighbors and also have a good working relationship. That's possible if both sides are professional, respectful, and fair. And both of us were; there was never a problem between us.

Moeller replaced Bo Schembechler as the head coach in 1990 and had five outstanding seasons before moving on to the NFL. Lloyd Carr, who had Moeller serve as the best man in his wedding, replaced Moeller as Michigan's head coach and led the Wolverines to their only national championship since 1948 in 1997 with a team sparked by Heisman Trophy winner Charles Woodson, a member of Moeller's last recruiting class.

Moeller, more than anybody, took the Michigan program to a level even Bo could not reach. He was a definite meat-and-potatoes kind of guy with simple needs and none of the flash that other top recruiting college coaches such as Jimmy Johnson and Steve Spurrier possessed. But Moeller still found a way to connect with elite athletes.

What in his approach allowed him to have that success?

"You just talk to 'em," Moeller said. "Hey, but I lost a lot of players, too."

Jerome Bettis, the Detroit Mackenzie running back, chose Notre Dame over Michigan. He was the best player Moeller ever lost, but he didn't lose many. However, Moeller did land an All-American running back that same season in Ricky Powers, and the next year he signed the most pivotal player he secured as a head coach.

Tyrone Wheatley, the 1993 Rose Bowl MVP who rushed for 4,178 yards for the Wolverines, had pretty much decided to attend Michigan State as a senior at Dearborn Heights (Michigan) Robichaud High in 1991.

But he lived only about a 30-minute drive from Ann Arbor and was coaxed by Moeller into taking a visit. In a one-on-one conversation with Moeller in his office and walking around Schembechler Hall, Wheatley found himself captivated with Moeller after spending over an hour with him.

"I just wanted to play for that man," Wheatley said of Moeller. He said Moeller was the only coach who wanted to go deeper than football with him, and that made all the difference. Wheatley became a Wolverine that day.

"Tyrone was a different kid," Moeller said. "He tried to help raise his brother and sister. He wanted to be a father figure to them, and he was proud of that. I just told him, 'You've got a big name, and you are a star. And you can come here and continue to be close to them. You'll get a very good education and an excellent degree.'

"I could tell his family meant everything to him. And hats off to Tyrone—he was and is such a trustworthy guy."

Charles Woodson, who was from Fremont, Ohio, spurned Ohio State to play for Moeller and Michigan. Despite rushing for more than 2,000 yards, Woodson chose to play cornerback on defense.

"We were recruiting Woodson on defense, and one night I got to thinking of a kid I lost to Ohio State named Mike Lanese," Moeller said. Lanese caught 72 passes for 1,170 yards for the Buckeyes, including a critical third-and-long reception from Mike Tomczak that secured OSU's 1984 win over Michigan.

"Lanese was a receiver-defensive back who we liked," Moeller added, "and Ohio State went after him as a receiver and we lost him. I started thinking, 'You know, Ohio State is going to go down there and tell Woodson he can be a running back, and we're going to lose him that way.' So one night I decided to give Woodson a call. I told him, 'I'm going to make you a running back.'"

Woodson had no hesitation in turning down that offer.

"He said, 'Uh-uh, I'm not playing running back,'" Moeller said. "You think you have it all figured out as the head coach."

Moeller chuckled, adding that he assured Woodson he could play cornerback.

"I reminded Charles of that when I saw him a few years ago," Moeller added. "I'll never forget that night because I was worried about losing him. But he just enjoyed playing cornerback most. Then when I wasn't coaching Michigan, I remember watching him make that one-handed interception against Michigan State that was just unbelievable."

Moeller was also the assistant coach in charge of recruiting Desmond Howard and his Cleveland St. Joseph High classmate, Elvis Grbac, for Michigan. They signed with Bo but flourished under Moeller in the pro-style offense he implemented along with quarterbacks coach Cam Cameron, who went on to become the head coach at Indiana University and briefly with the Miami Dolphins before serving as offensive coordinator of the Baltimore Ravens.

"Do you know that Elvis threw exactly one pass to Desmond in high school—exactly one?" Moeller said. "That team didn't throw much. Elvis threw 110 passes as a senior, but we knew he had the strong arm and was very accurate. He was a big-time basketball player and went to St. Joe to play that first before really getting into football. It was the same thing with Desmond. He was a great little point guard, and they went a long way in the state tournaments.

"I thought they'd be pretty good, but I'd be lying if I said I thought they would do what they did."

Elvis combined with Desmond to set NCAA records for most touchdowns by one quarterback completed to one receiver for a career (31) and single season (19) in 1991, when Desmond won the Heisman Trophy in a landslide vote. Grbac departed Michigan owning every major career passing record.

"Elvis was big and different from the other quarterbacks we'd had," Moeller said. "Was he heavily recruited? Probably not. But Purdue came in on him at the end and was our biggest competition for Elvis.

"It probably came down to Georgia Tech with Desmond. When he was inducted into the College Football Hall of Fame in South Bend, his mom said, 'I told this Moeller guy, I don't care about the football. I want this guy to get an education.' She liked Georgia Tech a lot. His dad, J.D., loved the football, and both had a big influence on him. And J.D. liked Michigan—he saw us as big-time college football."

However, the Elvis-to-Desmond combo almost never happened based on Desmond's original position choice. Moeller said Bo had a talk with the freshmen on the first day of practice, and then he had them separate into the offensive meeting room with Moeller or the defensive meeting room with Carr.

"I'm talking to the offense," said Moeller, then the coordinator on that side of the ball, "and I'm ready to say something to Desmond. But he's not in the room. I said, 'Where the heck is Desmond?' Somebody told me he was next door with the defense. I said, 'Well, get Desmond in here!' He comes into our room and says, 'I think I'm going to play cornerback.'"

Moeller could not believe it.

"I said, 'Your dad is going to shoot me, Desmond! I promised him you would play running back.' Desmond said, 'I just want to play early.' But I said, 'This is what you came here for—to play offense.' He didn't argue about it and stayed with the offense. Desmond was just so explosive when he caught the ball, and he wouldn't have to take as many hits as a receiver. But he was tough and could've played tailback like he did in high school."

Desmond was red-shirted as a freshman in 1988, and Moeller said J.D. had no problem with him playing receiver. "No, J.D. was happy," Moeller said. "He was very happy."

Desmond, Woodson, and Wheatley—perhaps the three most exciting players to wear the Maize and Blue in the last 50 years—were very much influenced by Moeller. You can debate whether Anthony Carter, Braylon Edwards, and Denard Robinson belong in their company, but there is no denying that Moeller put together brilliant football talent and teams.

Consider this:

Moeller was 44–13–4 for a .771 winning percentage that edged Carr (.763) and was just a shade below Bo's .802. Moeller won three Big Ten titles in five seasons; he went 4-for-5 in Bowl games while splitting a pair of Rose Bowls; and he was 3–1–1 against Ohio State.

Moeller also did something that none of the conference's coaching legends could match. His teams set the Big Ten's record for most consecutive conference wins at 19 with the blockbuster teams from 1990–92. Those teams were powered not only by outstanding skill position players but offensive linemen such as future NFL players Steve Everitt, Greg Skrepenak, Dean Dingman, Matt Elliott, and Tom Dohring. Those five players shared the 1990 Gator Bowl's MVP award.

Woody Hayes, for whom Moeller played and was a captain for as a Buckeyes linebacker, didn't win 19 straight. Neither did Wolverines coaching giants Fritz Crisler or Fielding H. Yost or his mentor, Bo Schembechler.

Moeller first met Bo at Ohio State when Bo was on Hayes' staff. They all won a national championship together in 1961 wearing Scarlet and Gray. Bo coached the offensive line, and Moeller played some center and guard as a two-way player.

"This might surprise everybody," Moeller said, "but Bo was the nice guy at Ohio State. He never got on anybody. Now, Woody would get all over everybody. But Bo didn't do that as an assistant. People would not believe how he changed and how aggressive Bo was when he started coaching at Miami and Michigan. I tell people, 'At Ohio State, Bo was the nice guy.' And they say, 'Really?'

"Now, it was not that Bo was not tough back then because he was. He was honest from the start, too. He had a very good way of getting on players at Michigan and still having a relationship with them. He always made it a point to talk to players he got on, but he did it without being soft. And that was important. He would go up to them calmly and say,

'This is important. Do you understand that?' But Bo would not carry a torch around about something and burn you every day with it."

"The greatest thing I got from Bo was watching him handle players. He knew how to motivate, discipline, and earn their trust. And they truly enjoyed playing for him because they knew he cared about them. He knew how to handle situations and was a good person. He had good teaching skills and was not afraid to stand up for what was right. And he was not afraid to get on the superstars. That, too, was important."

Moeller was on Bo's staff at Miami of Ohio in 1967 and 1968, and came with Bo to Ann Arbor in 1969 as the defensive ends coach. Moeller replaced defensive coordinator Jim Young, who took the Arizona head coaching job in 1972.

And by 1977, after having defenses that led the nation in scoring defense in 1974 and 1976, Moeller was hired as the head coach at Illinois. He was only 36, a "boy coach," when he first led the Illini. Bo was 34 when he got his first head coaching job at Miami in 1963 but didn't crack the Big Ten until he was 40.

But Illinois was a disaster for Moeller. His teams from 1977–79 went 6–24–3, and he was fired.

"We were recruiting a great player not far from the Illinois campus," said Carr, who was Moeller's defensive backs coach on the Fighting Illini. "He was a great running back who we really needed. Word came back to us that he was going to another school that offered to buy him a car. A big alumni member in Champaign said to Mo, 'Listen, I will take care of this and get this kid a car.'

"Now, we are going into our third year with a lot of pressure. And Mo says, 'We are not buying him a car. Forget that!' This guy withdrew [as a booster]. We didn't get the kid, had a bad season, and we got fired. He knew we needed that kid but would not sacrifice his integrity."

Bo, who fumed forever about Illinois not giving his prized pupil enough time, broke his own rule about bringing back assistants who left for Moeller. He returned as the quarterbacks coach at Michigan in 1980 and once again served as the defensive coordinator from 1982–87.

There was a scene from the visitors' locker room at Spartan Stadium in 1985, after a 31–0 domination in a very hostile environment against a strong offense, that was special. Moeller puffed a victory cigar in the steamy locker room. The mist and the smoke drifted over to where Bo was seated a few feet away.

Unless you like to smoke in saunas, it wasn't a comfortable combination. But it was a moment that provided the essence of savoring a complete and total victory over their intrastate rival, and Bo and Mo could not stop smiling through the haze. Everything feels good when you win and win big and stop a big running back.

Spartans tailback Lorenzo White ran for a Big Ten record 2,066 yards that season and finished fourth in Heisman Trophy voting. But in that game, White was limited to 47 yards on 18 carries. He had run for 226 yards the week before against No. 1 Iowa in Iowa City.

"They have a hard, tough defense," White said. "But we missed a couple blocks, too. I kept feeling I might break one. I feel we can come back on anybody. I would say Michigan was perhaps better prepared than Iowa for us."

Michigan State's freshman starting offensive tackle, Tony Mandarich, became a phenomenon. He was on the cover of *Sports Illustrated* in a story titled, "The Incredible Bulk," and I wrote a feature on him for *The Sporting News*. Mandarich was perhaps the most publicized blocker the game has ever known, and he lauded his unique diet and workout addiction for his power and speed. Mandarich weighed 304 lbs. yet ran a 4.65-second 40-yard dash as a senior. He bench-pressed 225 lbs. a Herculean 39 times in a set.

He was later revealed to be on steroids, and *SI* ran another cover story, "The NFL's Incredible Bust," after he failed miserably for the Green Bay Packers, who made Mandarich the second overall pick in the 1989 draft—right after Troy Aikman and right before Barry Sanders. But in that game against the Wolverines, he was no factor at all.

Moeller took the cigar out of his mouth, smiled, and said, "We couldn't allow White to get a crease to run to. So we had linebackers filling up the gaps. A back like White can make you miss, so the only way to stop him is with numbers. He's going to make you miss, but he's not going to make you miss on five guys in a row."

His inside linebackers, Mike Mallory and his son, Andy, were smart and tough. Outside linebackers Jeff Akers and Jim Scarcelli were quick and agile. Middle guard Billy Harris was a load to get around. But the difference-makers were a pair of relentless tackles, future All-Americans Mike Hammerstein and Mark Messner, who was just a freshman.

"What that defense did so well was get focused," Moeller said. "They were smart and allowed no big plays."

Moeller had another truly great defense—one that would once again lead the nation in scoring defense.

Andy followed his father into coaching and was the offensive line coach for the Baltimore Ravens when they won Super Bowl XLVII by a 34–31 score over the San Francisco 49ers, whose head coach was Andy's high school and college teammate, Jim Harbaugh.

"Me and Ann went to that game in New Orleans," Moeller said. "I was jumping up and down at the end, and Andy was looking up and signaling back and forth to us. My wife went crazy. It's hard to believe Andy won a Super Bowl ring. And then with Jimmy on the other side, that was something."

Andy has often spent the night at the Ravens' coaching offices, sleeping between film sessions. And he comes by that tendency honestly.

Gary Moeller never ceased to look for an edge on film. Ann told me that he took film with him on their annual summer vacation to a lake. He was good about spending the day on a pontoon boat, swimming with the kids, and grilling for dinner. He kept the film in his suitcase. But when Ann and the kids went someplace for a few hours and left him alone, Moeller popped in the film.

"I came back and found him stretched out on the floor there, watching film," Ann said. "He couldn't have been happier."

Moeller said, "I really enjoyed the strategy of the game. I could watch film all day and all night. I truly loved what I did."

Bo's assistants said that they would not dare leave the football building before he did during the season. He usually knocked off between 11:00 PM and midnight. But Moeller was one of those rare birds, like Bo, who didn't mind the long hours and had an insatiable appetite for football.

"Mo had a great passion for the game and everything it entailed," Carr said. "And he cared about the players so much. There is never a higher compliment than to say that."

In 1987, Bo switched Moeller to offensive coordinator. Carr became the defensive coordinator. Bo assured that Moeller would have everything needed in his background to succeed him.

Jim Brandstatter, the longtime radio analyst for Wolverines football and host of the *Michigan Replay* coaching television show for Bo, Moeller, and Carr, laughed about a sideline scene of Bo and Moeller arguing at the 1981 Rose Bowl. Moeller was the quarterbacks coach that season.

"I looked down and Bo was shooing Mo away," Brandstatter said. "Both of them were ticked off at each other about something. And on the next play, John Wangler threw a slant pass to Anthony Carter for a touchdown that was huge."

The seven-yard touchdown made it 17–6 for Michigan with three minutes left in the third quarter of a 23–6 victory that was Bo's first in Pasadena after five losses there on New Year's Day.

"Years later," Brandstatter said, "I asked Mo what the problem was before that touchdown. He said, 'I wanted to run it off tackle, and he wanted to throw it.' Bo told Mo that they could not cover Anthony on a slant route there. Who would've thought that Bo was the one arguing to pass? They were like co-offensive coordinators back then and went at it. But there was always that respect."

And Mo had great success in following a legend—which seldom occurs.

Years later, I was covering the Detroit Lions for the *Oakland Press* in Pontiac, Michigan, and Moeller was coaching linebackers for the Lions. We would meet every Friday afternoon after practice and interviews and talk about something we both loved—the football team at Ann Arbor Pioneer High.

My youngest sons, Brad and Derek, played there in a stadium kitty-corner from the Big House. And Brad was still playing at the time.

"What number does Brad wear?" Moeller asked.

I told him Brad wore No. 49.

Moeller's eyes got as big as saucers, and a smile creased his face.

"No kidding!" he said. "That was Andy's number, too. How did they do last week?"

One year at Lions training camp in Saginaw, Michigan, Moeller noticed that Brad had come up to watch practice before two-a-days began for Pioneer. He sought out my son and asked if he had brought his football cleats.

"They're in the trunk of my car," Brad said.

Moeller asked if he wanted to work out after that day's afternoon practice, and my son couldn't accept quickly enough.

They worked for about one hour on footwork and technique, and even got on the blocking sled. Brad was a tight end, but he also played some middle linebacker. He told me that he learned more in that short tutorial with Moeller than he had in all the previous football practices he had attended.

Hayes pounded a pay-it-forward principle into his players and coaches, and Moeller was following through on a lesson he'd been taught nearly 40 years prior. But he was also following through on being a good neighbor, and that is how I remember him most. And that is how the folks on Maywood viewed him, too. After Michigan beat Washington in the 1993 Rose Bowl, I noticed something funny hanging on the street sign off Stadium Boulevard as I jogged toward it. Somebody had printed "Mo-wood" on cardboard and rigged it over the aluminum street sign.

Those were the best of days for Moeller. I never believed that the national media or even Michigan fans appreciated all that he did. But then, Gary Moeller didn't coach for anybody but his assistants and players. And he impacted some of the greatest players the school has ever had.

That was enough for Mo.

Ann and Gary Moeller have long since moved away from Maywood. They now live the good life in a house on a lake just north of Ann Arbor in Hamburg.

I asked what he was proudest of from his time at Michigan.

"Upsetting Ohio State in '69," Moeller said. "I don't think you can ever beat that. But from when I was the head coach, I'd have to say it was winning the Rose Bowl." Grbac's 15-yard touchdown pass to tight end Tony McGee finished off a 38–31 comeback win over Washington in Pasadena on January 1, 1993.

"Winning that game was so important for the players on that team to get recognized," Moeller said. "My favorite moment was watching all the players sing 'The Victors' with our fans and the band. That's what it's all about, really the kids. And that's what it was all about for me."

CHAPTER 14

Steve Everitt:
Surviving a Shattered Jaw and Hurricane Andrew

If I had to pick one Michigan football player to throw the block on the biggest play of the game, I would choose center Steve Everitt. And if I had to pick one Wolverine to accompany me down a dark alley on the south side of Chicago, I would choose Everitt.

You want imposing? You want swag? You want results? He's your guy.

Everitt remains intimidating. You will see him during TV shots on the sidelines in Ann Arbor at big games—always the Ohio State games. He is pretty hard to miss. Everitt still looks like he's in playing shape, has a ZZ Top beard, and is wearing a backward baseball cap, shorts, and a "BIG HOUSE FOOTBALL" T-shirt. Picture the "Big Lebowski" as a football player, and you've got Everitt.

He looks like he could still play, and you get the idea the thought has crossed his mind. There is an urgency and fire in Everitt's eyes at such games that normally fades from most players when they return to cheer on their alma maters. But he always had that look and probably always will.

When the Wolverines broke the huddle and Everitt surveyed his opponents before bending over to grip the football, he seemed to be saying, "You want a piece of this?"

In 1991, in a game in which Michigan beat the Buckeyes 31–3 to complete an undefeated Big Ten season in Michigan Stadium, I spoke to

Everitt afterward. He began to laugh and told me that Ohio State defensive end Alonzo Spellman talked unbelievable trash during the game.

"So what did you come back with?" I asked.

Everitt said, "I pointed up beyond the end zone and said, 'Look at the scoreboard, stupid.'" Although, he probably didn't say it quite so nicely.

A smile creased Everitt's face, and he shook his head. Then he chuckled in that slow, counted chuckle of his. His eyes twinkled, and he took a deep breath.

"Spellman looked up at the scoreboard," Everitt said, "but he didn't shut up."

It came out years later that Spellman, who would be drafted eight picks after Everitt in the first round five months later, suffered from bipolar disorder and had run-ins with the law. On that day, he refused to acknowledge the domination of what was Michigan's widest margin of victory in "The Game" since a 58–6 win in 1946. And it has not won by more since.

The Wolverines won a conference-record 19 consecutive Big Ten games during Everitt's sophomore, junior, and senior seasons. At the center of this success was a dominating offensive line, perhaps the best to ever play together at a school with a tradition of producing great NFL linemen such as Dan Dierdorf, Mike Kenn, and Steve Hutchinson.

Everitt started on Wolverines lines with three All-American guards—Dean Dingman, Matt Elliott, and Joe Cocozzo—and one All-American tackle, Greg Skrepenak. And he started with four other NFL draft pick linemen—tight ends Tony McGee and Derrick Walker and tackles Tom Dohring and Doug Skene.

I called them the "Block M," and line coaches Jerry Hanlon, Les Miles, and Mike DeBord formed them into something special.

While at the *Detroit Free Press*, I had once had the offensive line starting unit pose together on the steps of the University of Michigan Museum of Art. They created something of a commotion in doing so, these 300-pounders wearing the same football team blazers and ties they wore on road trips. Several students stopped to watch the photo shoot, and one of them had a snazzy red bicycle. Everitt started a conversation with the bike's owner and asked questions about it. Our photographer, Pauline Lubens, took a shot of the linemen standing in front of the towering concrete columns of the museum with Everitt sitting on the red bike.

That made the photo—which Coach Gary Moeller had framed and hung prominently in his office at Schembechler Hall.

Everitt was the comic relief of the group, and he could be pretty quirky.

Elliott said the team once had a Spring Break theme for winter conditioning. "We were supposed to come one day in beachwear," Elliott said. "Everitt and Bill Schaffer showed up wearing lime-green string bikinis. The fellas about peed their pants."

Then there were the below-freezing temperatures during which he went for a runs sans shirt. And the times he did his impersonations of Moeller and defensive tackle Mike Evans, complete with his Jamaican accent. He once went hunting with Cocozzo in New York and fell asleep in a tree while holding a .30-06 rifle only to fall from the perch and knock the wind out of himself.

Skrepenak said, "The kid is practically nuts. An elephant ran on the screen once in a team movie and he yelled from the back, 'SKRRRREPENAK!' Everyone laughed; I laughed. He does stuff like that all the time. Steve keeps the monotony at a minimum and is a steady stream of fun."

He also had an adventurer's soul. When the team was at the Rose Bowl during his freshman year, Everitt just had to climb to the HOLLYWOOD sign, located near Mullholland Drive in Griffith Park on Mount Lee, the highest point in Los Angeles. He made it up to those 45' white letters along with teammates John Woodlock and Paul Manning.

"Woody, Manny, and myself were driving around Hollywood as

freshmen with a map of the stars' homes," Everitt said. "We couldn't find any but ended up where that HOLLYWOOD sign is.

"It only looked five minutes away but it took us two hours to scale this 89-degree incline. I slipped 20' once and almost flew off the side. I thought I was going to die. But we got up there and hung on the letters, tried to knock them down. Then we couldn't get down. We started hearing coyotes."

His father, Michael, said, "These are things that only happen to Steven. He is a magnet for weird stuff."

But somehow he found his way down from the HOLLYWOOD hill without an injury, which would have been one of the strangest to ever keep a player out of the granddaddy of them all, the Rose Bowl.

Not that any injury short of broken limbs would have kept Everitt off that field or any field.

Longtime Michigan football trainer Russ Miller said Everitt and middle linebacker Mike Mallory, the two-time captain in 1984 and 1985, were by far the two toughest players he had ever worked with. "You would have to cut their leg off to keep them out," Miller said.

A broken jaw was something that Everitt didn't want to keep him from missing even one game.

In the second quarter of the 1991 Notre Dame game, while engaging in trench warfare with Pete Bercich, the Fighting Irish linebacker, Bercich's helmet drove upward and under Everitt's faceguard. The odds of such a direct hit to the chin on a player with a helmet are slim to none, but slim happened. Everitt's jaw was shattered in several places.

"I remember looking into his eyes on the field," said current LSU coach Les Miles, then one of Michigan's offensive line coaches, "and there he was with his jaw busted, teeth knocked out, and blood spewing everywhere, saying, 'I'll be okay.'

"It was the worst injury I've ever seen, and later with his jaw wired together, he was still talking."

Three titanium plates were inserted into the jaw to stabilize it.

Early the following week, I called Everitt. I knew his parents had stayed to take care of him for a few days and would answer his phone. His parents were very friendly folks. Barb was a ninth grade English teacher, and Michael was an artist. Steve was a lot like him and graduated from Michigan with a bachelor of fine arts degree. He worked in watercolors, sculpture, computer-generated art, and drawings in pen, ink, pencil, and charcoal.

Barb picked up the phone and told me, "Steven was drinking milkshakes." And he was feeling better. She thanked me for calling to check in on her son, and said, "Steven wants to talk to you."

I laughed and said, "That's okay. There's no way he should be talking with a busted-up jaw. But I appreciate that. Tell him I said hello and to get better."

She said, "No, he said he really wants to talk to you. I'm going to put him on the line."

Everitt grabbed the phone and abruptly said, "I want to play." Only it was a little hard to make out because he sounded like the Mush Mouth character Bill Cosby worked into his comedy bits about growing up in North Philadelphia.

"What?" I asked. "You're kidding, right?"

He repeated, "I want to play. I'm okay."

Everitt went to Miami Southridge High and wanted badly to play in the next game against a powerhouse Florida State team, which was chock full of players Everitt played against in high school or knew of. The bye week between the Irish and the Seminoles gave him 14 days between games, but the team physicians wouldn't let him play in the game. It killed him, but that's the way it was.

"When you talk about tough," Tyrone Wheatley told me, "you have to talk about beyond tough where Steve Everitt is concerned. There was the time when he broke his right [thumb] and had it casted. He learned how to snap left-handed and came right back. I witnessed this and still can't believe it."

Hiking lefty against Purdue coming off that injury, he only messed up one snap.

Wheatley, the 1993 Rose Bowl MVP, ran through holes created by Everitt in his first two seasons at Michigan.

"And then with that broken jaw," Wheatley continued. "They wired his jaw, and one of the wires broke. There was blood all over, but he continued to play."

He missed only one game with the jaw, but an ankle injury caused Everitt to miss four more starts that season. As tough as Everitt was, injuries cost him basically one season's worth of games at Michigan. And it cost the Wolverines when he was on the sideline. They were 29–3–3 (.871) when he started and 9–4 (.692) when he did not. They averaged 6.2 yards per carry in games he started, and 4.4 yards per carry when he did not. That's a staggering difference.

One of those games he did not start, but was able to play in, was the disappointing Rose Bowl loss to Washington coming off Desmond Howard's Heisman Trophy win.

That season, I asked Desmond, "If you needed one block to spring you in the biggest play of a game, who would you want throwing that block?"

He didn't hesitate. "Steve Everitt."

And all these years later, I still agree with Desmond.

Those injuries cost Everitt All-America selection in 1991, and he also fell short of that honor in 1992. West Virginia's Mike Compton was named on the vast majority of the '92 teams—including the Associated Press and United Press International teams. And Iowa's Mike Devlin was named by the American Football Coaches Association and the Football Writers Association of America teams.

Everitt's reward came in the NFL draft that April. He was the first center and first interior lineman selected, going 14th overall in the first round to the Cleveland Browns. Compton went in the third round to the Detroit Lions as an offensive guard, and Devlin was taken in the fifth round by the Buffalo Bills.

Hurricane Andrew Took Everything but Their Lives, Dogs, and Gator Bowl MVP Trophy

Everitt did not know what became of his family when Hurricane Andrew ravaged the Cutler Ridge community he grew up in south of Miami. So when the Everitts called the football offices once they made their way to a phone, the fact that his family was calling was relayed down to the practice field along State Street. Moeller told Everitt he had a phone call and was excused.

His parents, younger sister Amy, and the two family dogs, both German shepherds, had survived Andrew. They stayed in their home rather than evacuate as authorities advised and squeezed into a bathtub to survive the frightening ordeal while everything they owned blew away. Oh, they kept one thing. Steve's 1990 Gator Bowl MVP trophy went in the tub with them.

People outside of the hurricane-prone states generally shake their heads and question why people in them stay with danger headed their way. I know because I used to think that. Then while living in Tampa Bay, Hurricane Charley became the rare storm that didn't hit the Atlantic Ocean coast or head toward the Florida Panhandle, Louisiana, or Texas. The eye of the storm was predicted to be Tarpon Springs, about 10 miles north of where I lived in Palm Harbor. And I stayed with about half the people in my subdivision, hoping it changed course and making the ill-advised decision to make a run for it late in the game if it did not. But dramatically, about four hours before reaching land, that Category 4 Hurricane in 2004 jogged south and decimated Punta Gorda.

Andrew, the Category 5 Hurricane with its 165-mph winds, made landfall just south of Cutler Ridge before the sun came up on August 24, 1992. It ripped apart Homestead, killed 23 people, and did $25 billion in damage according to the National Oceanic and Atmospheric Administration files. Andrew was just the third Category 5 to hit United States soil, but the Everitts were able to move on from its fury and wrath.

Barb called me some weeks after the storm to say that all of her son's scrapbooks had been blown miles away, perhaps as far as the Everglades. She asked if I could help recover some of the stories I'd written about him. Laurie Delves, who made so many good things happen behind the scenes in the *Free Press* sports department, got some editors on it. And in a few days, a package full of stories was sent to Cutler Ridge.

I flew down to Miami the day before the NFL draft on April 25, 1993, to write about their remarkable survival and recovery and about how their son was about to become a millionaire nearly eight months to the day after Andrew.

Here's what I wrote:

> Television provided Steve Everitt two emotional scenes this year.
>
> There was the morning of August 24, when he turned on CNN to view the destruction Hurricane Andrew wrought on his neighborhood.
>
> "CNN showed the Holiday Inn just five blocks from our house, and it was destroyed," Mike Everitt said. "It looked like Beirut and scared Steven something awful. He wondered what had happened to us."
>
> Then there was Sunday afternoon, when Everitt and his family and friends watched ESPN to learn for whom he would play in the NFL.
>
> The Cleveland Browns had called minutes before the TV announcement to say they were drafting him in the first round, 14th overall, but it wasn't official. So after hanging up with the Browns, he crouched in front of the tube and gazed intensely at it.
>
> When NFL commissioner Paul Tagliabue announced, "The Cleveland Browns select Steve Everitt," the room erupted with joy. Everyone hugged and smiled, and minutes later there was a champagne toast to the future.
>
> It might be a rich one.

The No. 14 selection last year, New York Giants tight end Derek Brown, signed a four-year deal with a $1.5 million bonus and $960,000 annual salary.

The nightmare of eight months ago had transformed into a dream come true. Everitt became the first center taken in the first round since the Los Angeles Rams picked Washington's Bern Brostek in 1990.

"I remember how down I was last year at this time," Everitt said. "I had the broken jaw and then the injury before the Rose Bowl, and it was a bad snowball all the way to the hurricane. Things just kept getting worse.

"But after that, life began falling back into place. The season just got better and better, and the good things didn't stop until today. This was the culmination."

When the Browns first called, he talked briefly and then glanced from the kitchen to where his mother, Barb, was seated in the family room. He smiled and pointed to himself, a signal that the Browns were taking him.

Barb quickly grabbed the Browns cap Steve had been given by the team on his tour of Cleveland last week. The celebrating began, but Steve said, "It's premature; it's not legal yet."

The smile on his face said otherwise.

He knew there was a chance the Browns would take him after they traded No. 1 picks (11th for 14th) with the Denver Broncos, but Illinois tackle Brad Hopkins had to go No. 13 to the Philadelphia Eagles for that to happen. Cleveland coveted Hopkins and had Everitt next on its wish list.

Everitt paced in front of the TV before the Eagles picked. He looked up at the ceiling and extended both arms, saying, "Please take Hopkins."

When they took Hopkins, Everitt said, "YES!" His father shouted for joy. The phone rang.

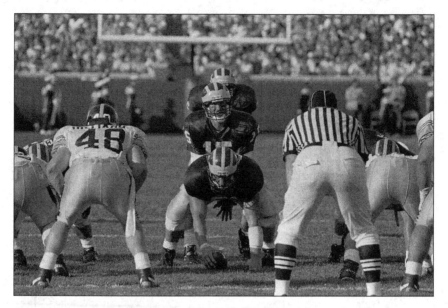

Center Steve Everitt prepares to snap the ball to Wolverine quarterback Elvis Grbac (15) against Iowa Hawkeye Matt Hilliard (48) in Ann Arbor, Michigan, on October 3, 1992. Everitt was picked by the Cleveland Browns in the first round of the 1993 NFL Draft in New York. (AP Photo/Bill Waugh)

It was the Browns.

Everitt purposely limited the number of people watching with him to three friends, a reporter, his parents, and sister Amy. He wanted to feel comfortable amid the uncertainty, but he was still obviously on edge.

Every once in a while something funny happened to take his mind off it. Like when the neighborhood Avon lady came knocking.

"I told her she would have to come back because the NFL draft was going," Barb said, "and she said, 'I hope your son's team wins.'"

Mike said: "That puts all this in perspective."

There is perspective all up and down Lenaire Drive. Eight months ago, an "UNFIT FOR HUMAN HABITATION" sign was affixed to most homes and troops carrying M-16 rifles patrolled the streets to discourage looters.

Amy, Barb, Mike, and their two German shepherds had curled up in the bathroom with Steve's Gator Bowl trophy and survived the hurricane.

Now they were together, healthy, and happy. Much of the rebuilding is completed, and their son will soon be a millionaire.

"It's ironic that Steven and I have the same favorite artist, Salvador Dali," Mike said, "because surreal is the only way to describe this year."

And that was the end of that story and their eight-month odyssey from the path of destruction to the path of gold.

Mike asked me to write my story in Steve's room rather that drive one hour back to my hotel. That way we could have dinner that night. He hated flying and was letting Barb accompany Steve on a flight that night to Cleveland for a press conference. Steve asked me to help him pick between his two ties while he got dressed, and I wrote on my laptop at his bedroom desk. We laughed because we both hate wearing ties.

It was a nice ending to that chapter of their lives, and Barb sent me a Christmas card that year to thank me for what I had done for her son over the years. But Steve and his parents did so much more for me with their hospitality and friendship.

Steve played eight years in the NFL for the Browns, Baltimore Ravens, Philadelphia Eagles, and St. Louis Rams. He started 98 of the 103 games he played before leaving the league with painful neck and back injuries. Everitt retired, got married, and was spending his time fishing and painting in the Florida Keys, according to a 2007 article in the *Baltimore Sun*.

But he continued to be an individualist in the social confines of the NFL. Everitt claimed to have not had a haircut since 1991. He wore his long blond hair in a ponytail before other players were doing so, and he hosted a weekly heavy-metal radio show at 98 Rock in Baltimore.

Everitt loved playing for the Browns and their gritty fans in the Dawg Pound. He even lived in Cleveland when he played there, soaking up life in the Rock and Roll Hall of Fame city. Everitt loved the raucous stage act and music of KISS almost as much as Michigan football, and he had come to identify himself with Cleveland, as well.

And he pledged allegiance to the Browns once owner Art Modell moved them to Baltimore to become the Ravens in 1996. Mike Klingaman of the *Baltimore Sun* wrote that Everitt had a "dagger tattooed down his spine to symbolize the knife in the back that Everitt felt Cleveland got from owner Art Modell." And at halftime of the Ravens' first game, he took off his helmet to expose a Browns bandana. The league fined him $5,000 for that gesture.

Everitt was the best blocker I saw in my years of covering the Wolverines and easily the most unique personality, too. I miss the guy. I really do.

CHAPTER 15

Elvis Grbac:
The American Dream

I stood outside the Michigan locker room at the Rose Bowl and could hear the joy as teammates exalted in triumph. The hoots, hollers, and songs of victory echoed off the walls and through the high ventilation windows. There was usually silence in that room when the Wolverines came to Pasadena, but not this time. Not after a comeback 38–31 win over Washington on January 1, 1993. Tyrone Wheatley ran for 235 yards, and Elvis Grbac's 15-yard touchdown pass to tight end Tony McGee was the game-winner.

The Wolverines were stoked. They were pumped. And back in the stadium, Grbac had borrowed the band director's baton to take a shot at orchestrating "The Victors" as well as he had a victory.

It was the kind of game players never forget.

But it was the reaction of one of their parents that left the greatest impression. While standing there outside the locker room, running questions for the players through my head, I was suddenly engulfed by a giant bear hug from behind. I turned to see that it was Ivan Grbac, a very proud father with a message to deliver.

"This is the *American* dream!" Ivan proclaimed, tears rolling down the cheeks of his smiling face. "You know what we have come from! This is the American dream, the American dream. Oh, I can't believe it."

Elvis had hugged his father at midfield and emerged from the celebration with the game ball. He sprinted to the locker room, holding the game ball high all the way. "I've got it in my equipment bag, and I'm giving it to my dad," Elvis said. "He can put it on the mantel of our new home in Willoughby Hills [Ohio]. I saw how excited he was and how much this meant to Dad."

His father was overcome with emotion from the get-go. "I cried when they sang the 'National Anthem,'" Ivan said. "This is the American dream. I cried when they sang 'The Victors.' These five years have been so great for Elvis. I cried when we hugged after the game. I was so happy for my son, so proud."

I shook Ivan's hand and agreed that his son's final college performance after a record-setting career was the perfect ending to a story that began when Ivan and Cecilia Grbac left their native Croatia for religious freedom and came to call football-crazy Cleveland their home.

That summer, I had watched as Ivan turned the yellowed pages of a family photo album to a picture that captured the flow of life. There, seated on a donkey, was his youngest son, Elvis, age 4, being led down a road by Ivan's father, Jacob Grbac. It was a scene from 18 summers prior in the farming village of Lanisce, located in northern Croatia and 25 miles from the Adriatic Sea.

"Everyone says I look most like my grandpa Jacob," said Elvis, seated across the dining room table from his father at their home in Willoughby Hills. Jacob died several years before his homeland was ripped wide open by a civil war and before his grandson on the donkey became one of college football's best quarterbacks at Michigan.

So much had changed since that sunny summer day nearly two decades ago—some for the better and some for the worse. Cecilia and Ivan Grbac were living that American dream. They moved into a spacious home they built on a peaceful, wooded court near a golf course. Their son Engelbert worked as an aviation mechanic, and daughter Maria was a nurse. Youngest daughter Barbara was entertaining a future as a major college basketball player, and Elvis was headed to an eight-year career in the NFL.

Quarterback Elvis Grbac looks for an open receiver during first-half action against Washington at the Rose Bowl in Pasadena, California, on January 1, 1993. Grbac completed 17-of-30 passes for 175 yards in the 38-31 Michigan win. (AP Photo/Bob Galbraith)

They were a family with much to smile about.

But at the same time, they picked up the newspaper or watched the TV news and saw their ravaged homeland and the malnourished Croatians in Serbian detention camps.

"I look at it now," Cecilia said then, in interviews I did for the *Detroit Free Press*, "and I say, 'Oh, my God!' But we know they must stay and fight for what they have."

Elvis added, "We know the country is not being run right, and we understand the history of hatred between Croatia and Serbia. But they have always lived a simple life of hard work, a family-oriented survival. And that will continue."

The Grbacs were thankful that their village, located in a mountain valley off the Alps range, was not a battle site. But the economic plight was everywhere in the country. "My three brothers there are engineers who made $300 a month," Cecilia said, "and now that is $60 a month. The food they raise to get by, but we send money and clothing. They say, 'If we did not have you in America, we would be so poor.'"

Ivan's only brother still lived in Croatia. "We will go back when I retire," Ivan said. "We will be there some, here some."

Emotion shook his voice. The Grbacs had nearly moved back six years prior when Elvis was a sophomore at Cleveland St. Joseph High.

"I guess I just would've had to be a good soccer or basketball player," Elvis said. "When we went there when I was 16, that's all the kids did for fun was play those two sports."

As long as he could be playing some game somewhere, he reasoned, he would've been happy. "I have shot baskets for hours in the rain," Elvis said. "It's what relaxes me. I take off sometimes on a run after midnight just because it feels right. And I don't want company. That is my way of getting away from my family.

"Athletics is my job, but it's one I love. If you love and cherish what you do, you can strive to be the best. It's why, though I am a nonchalant college student, I am a perfectionist with football. It's like my dad and his homes."

Ivan owned Grbac Construction Co., building Tudors and colonials in suburban Cleveland. I asked him about his employees. "There is just one," he said, holding up a finger. "It's me. And Cecilia does the paperwork and handles the telephone calls. She also stains and paints in the homes."

The Grbacs left Croatia in 1967 with their two eldest children, seeking the freedom to practice Catholicism and a life free from communist rule. And now they lived in a lovely four-bedroom home with a study, living room, dining room, family room, and a hot tub in the master bathroom.

More important, they had four children, all of whom absorbed their parents' example of self-reliance and character. As they gathered around the dining room table, along with Elvis and his future wife, Lori Immarino, each recalled a favorite story about the family football star.

Maria recalled the strange game of garage baseball when Elvis was eight. "He pitched a *Reader's Digest* for a ball, and I swung a tomato stake as a bat," she said. "The stake broke in half and spun right at him, hitting him between the eyes. There was blood all over, and he still has a scar from it."

Cecilia's story came from the same trip when Elvis and his grandfather were photographed. "Elvis has always been throwing things," she said, "and he threw a rock at a chicken and killed one. His grandmother just laughed and said she had to kill one for dinner anyway."

Elvis said, "But she made me get down on my knees and pray, saying I was sorry for killing it."

He leaned back in the chair and smiled, adding, "It was 10 to 15 yards away, and I hit it perfectly."

He was a quarterback at four, admiring what could happen by airing out his arm toward a moving target. It all started with a chicken, and by the time Elvis was 10, he made the paper for the first time by throwing a no-hitter in baseball. The arm attracted U-M coach Gary Moeller, then an assistant to Bo Schembechler, and convinced them to give scholarships to this raw quarterback and his elusive high school teammate, Desmond Howard.

He combined with Desmond to set NCAA records for most touchdowns by one quarterback completed to one receiver for a career (31) and single season (19) in 1991, when Desmond won the Heisman Trophy in a landslide vote.

Grbac departed Michigan owning every major career passing record. And his 522 completions for 6,460 yards and 71 touchdowns stood until John Navarre (2000–03) and current record-holder Chad Henne (2004–07) surpassed him.

Alumni and booster group members called me to complain after Bo awarded those scholarships to Elvis and Desmond. They were not All-Americans or on anybody's blue chip lists. And even Bo had to be convinced by Moeller—especially in the case of Elvis—to take them.

Doubters were nothing new where Elvis was concerned.

"I remember in high school when a lady sat in front of me at one of Elvis' games and was upset with how he played," Cecilia said. "She said, 'This kid will never be nothing.' I turned red but said nothing."

Elvis was seen as too slow a-foot, and he ended up losing 239 yards on 80 carries with just one touchdown (albeit an important one in his final regular season game at Ohio State in 1992) while wearing the Maize and Blue.

Bo favored nimble quarterbacks. Even Jim Harbaugh, his first NFL impact quarterback, could do a decent job of running the option. But Bo preferred guys like Dennis Franklin, Rick Leach, Michael Taylor, and Demetrius Brown, who could really run. Moeller was willing to build an offense around his quarterback, and Elvis was the first in a long line of future NFL stars who couldn't run the option but could zip out-cut passes and throw deep post patterns.

There was a slant and fade combination route that Grbac would throw to Desmond and Derrick Alexander, another longtime NFL receiver, that became Moeller's goal-line offense rather than the wishbone that Bo used in that situation in his later years.

But there was something about Elvis that got Bo to warm up to him before he retired as coach. One day I was sitting in Bo's old office at the corner of State and Hoover when he stood up and saw Elvis trudging around Ferry Field's rubber track below on a hot July afternoon.

"That guy," Bo said, "is going to be our quarterback. That guy is a leader."

The Grbacs never knew just how far this foreign game of football, of which they disapproved at first, might take Elvis. And it was his following of their old-world work ethic that had much to do with his success

ELVIS IMPERSONATOR

There are plenty of Elvis impersonators. But prior to the 1989 Rose Bowl, Michigan had Elvis the impersonator. Elvis Grbac, as a freshman quarterback, played the part of Southern Cal quarterback Rodney Peete, the Heisman Trophy runner-up, in practices leading up to their game.

I spoke with Elvis for the first time outside the Newporter Hotel in Newport Beach, California, to discuss his role. "I just try to run USC's plays by rolling out or faking and sometimes running back," Elvis said. "I watch film of Peete and try to simulate him as closely as possible."

But what I really wanted to ask him about was his name and if he had been named for Elvis Presley. "I don't know," Elvis said. "My brother's name is Engelbert. Sometimes people mock me, but most people just call me El. Yes, I've asked my parents how I got the name."

His face turned red and he added that his older brother was named for singer Engelbert Humperdinck. "I believe those names are really popular in Yugoslavia," Elvis explained.

Yugoslavia would dissolve in the years ahead when Croatia fought and won its independence during a war fought from 1991-95.

"My parents could not speak a word of English when they came here," Elvis said. "They had no money and had to work hard every day."

Listening to the songs of Elvis and Engelbert helped them learn the language and led to the names of their sons.

playing it. But no one figured football would take Elvis as far as it did.

Which brings us to the father's favorite story about his youngest son.

"It was 1989," Ivan said. "We had just started building this house, and Elvis was a redshirt freshman. Cecilia was going to the Notre Dame game, but I stayed because I figured he wouldn't play."

But then Taylor was hurt, and Bo passed over Wilbur Odom and Ken Sollom, a pair of All-American high school players from Texas and California, for the green kid nobody knew much about.

Ivan said, "A neighbor came running out, shouting, 'Ivan! Ivan! Elvis threw a TD!' I did not believe it, so I went in to watch the TV. I went back to work and he comes running back, shouting, 'Ivan! Elvis threw another TD!'"

"And so now I miss nothing. I see every game."

The carpenter from Croatia and the quarterback from Cleveland both came a long way to realize the American dream.

I thought of how proud Grandpa Jacob would be. And I thought of what immigrants leave behind to chase their dreams. I thought of my own father, who had died two weeks before Elvis' final game in Pasadena and was the son of a Polish immigrant who never learned more than a few words of English.

My father had lived the American dream that Elvis' father craved, and so I could very much relate to the words of Ivan Grbac outside the Rose Bowl locker room. The circle of life had connected as surely as his son's pass had connected with the game on the line.

CHAPTER 16

Tyrone Wheatley:
From Superman to Family Man

Tyrone Wheatley had electric eyes that locked onto you when you talked to him. And he had this boundless, kinetic energy that he unleashed at the drop of a hat…or in this case, the drop of a pillow.

The Wolverines had just finished watching their team movie the night before the 1994 Holiday Bowl game with Colorado State in San Diego, and the players made their way to the elevators of the Hyatt Regency in LaJolla, California.

I was standing at the elevators with my family after returning from dinner. Down the spacious hallway was Wheatley, breaking into a sprint and flopping onto his pillow as if it were a sled. He coasted through the lobby to the elevator doors.

Everybody laughed and shook their heads.

This was the night before his last game as a Wolverine, and I thought back to the first time I'd seen the three-sport star from Dearborn Heights (Michigan) Robichaud playing basketball. He could dunk with the Fab Five players who became his friends at Michigan, and he put on a show by living above the rim and powerfully slamming balls through the net. And he beamed while running down court afterward to set up on defense.

They called him "Superman" in high school, and nobody thought that was a hyperbolic tag. He was that sensational, that breathtaking.

Wheatley continued that vibrancy as a track and field All-American and All-Big Ten tailback wearing the Maize and Blue. He maintained

Tyrone Wheatley runs in for a second-quarter touchdown on a 56-yard run against Washington at the Rose Bowl in Pasadena, California, on January 1, 1993. (AP Photo/Bob Galbraith)

a flair for the dramatic—running for 235 yards with touchdown runs of 88, 56, and 24 yards as the 1993 Rose Bowl MVP—and was the Big Ten's Offensive Player of the Year and rushing leader with 1,357 yards as a sophomore in 1992.

And in that Rose Bowl game that elevated him to superstar status, he played most of it with one good leg. He could barely feel his left foot, experiencing numbness after a first-quarter helmet hit in the back. But he played through tingling and spasms and went to the sideline when Washington had the ball for stretching, ice and heat treatments.

Against Ohio State the next season, in 1993, after rushing for 105 yards in the first half, Wolverines running backs coach Fred Jackson had to confiscate Wheatley's helmet to keep him from running onto the field after an injury.

Wheatley was so tantalizing because he was a track star with size (6'1", 225 pounds), linebacker toughness, and what Penn State coach Joe Paterno called one of the best stiff-arms he'd ever seen in college football.

Only two players in Big Ten history had rushed for more than Wheatley's 47 touchdowns, and his 4,178 yards were just 215 yards short of Jamie Morris' school record at the time.

The New York Giants drafted him in the first round in 1995, but he reached 1,000 yards only once in 10 seasons with the Giants and Oakland Raiders. He finished with a modest 3.9 yards-per-carry average, 4,962 yards, and 40 rushing touchdowns.

How had a truly special player become such a pedestrian performer?

"I was not nifty," Wheatley said. "I was just a big guy who could run and run downhill. And that didn't work because in this league the guys were just as big and fast as me."

He's now the running backs coach for the Buffalo Bills, and he spoke to me on the phone from his office. Wheatley now realizes running backs must understand how to evolve and read keys properly, and said early in his career he "didn't really have a coach that helped me put those things together."

Wheatley had some injuries in the NFL but nothing debilitating. However, he did fall asleep in Giants team meetings and was often tardy. Something was lacking at that point in time. Though he was definitely happier playing for the Raiders and head coach Jon Gruden and running backs coach Skip Peete.

"Jon Gruden and Skip Peete tied it all together for me," Wheatley said. "But for me, my peak years ended up being short."

I was struck by the distant look in his eyes and languid body language upon meeting him on Super Bowl media day in San Diego in January 2003. Where had his aura and charisma gone? The NFL had apparently become a job and had worn him down, robbing him of his once ever-present joy of playing a primal game.

I was writing and editing for the *Tampa Tribune* and covering the Tampa Bay Buccaneers, but I looked forward to reconnecting with Wheatley, a Raiders reserve. He had little interest in seeing me again, however, and I didn't stay long at his interview station. Not all reunions are back-slappers.

I asked him about what he was feeling on that elevated platform that day.

"It was very painful," Wheatley said.

He'd never envisioned getting to the Super Bowl as a spare part.

He got his one and only Super Bowl carry several days later, picking up five yards as Oakland got blown out by the Bucs.

"Over time," Wheatley said, "I came to realize that Barry Sanders, the greatest runner of all time, never got one carry in the Super Bowl. And Walter Payton didn't get a touchdown. I may have had only that one carry, but many great players never got one."

And after two more laborious seasons, the formerly dominant and entertaining performer hung up his helmet.

It made me think back to something several former Wolverines told me after long NFL careers: "You know, the old man [Bo] told us that no matter what we did in the NFL, nothing would compare to the years we played together at Michigan." Then each of them would nod and add, "He was right."

But the NFL made Wheatley a millionaire, as it has countless Wolverines, and that set him up to do whatever he wanted after retiring. He chose to stay in football even though it required working his way up from internships and small college coaching positions. Becoming a lunch-pail player in the pros did not rob him of his love for the game.

Wheatley revitalized the football program at his alma mater, Dearborn Heights Robichaud. His head coach there, Bob Yauck, had inspired Wheatley to become a coach by watching Yauck impact lives and receive love from two generations of players. Wheatley then became an assistant coach at Ohio Northern, Eastern Michigan, and Syracuse. He returned to the NFL in 2013 with the Bills.

His goal is to become a head coach in the NFL or college, and Wheatley is off to a good start on his new dream. He's made the jump from college to the pros once again, and this time he has a whistle around his neck.

Wheatley could have gone to the NFL one year earlier as a player, but he surprised everyone by opting to play his fourth season in Ann Arbor. Wolverines offensive tackle Taylor Lewan made a similarly shocking choice by returning for his senior season in 2013 despite being a near lock to be taken in the first five picks.

One influence on Wheatley's decision was a conversation he had with Michigan basketball star Chris Webber, who left school after two years to become the No. 1 overall pick in the NBA draft by the Orlando Magic and was traded to the Golden State Warriors.

Webber told Wheatley that for all the riches and fame the NBA brought him, if he had it to do over again, he would have spent one more year with Jalen Rose, his childhood friend from Detroit, and those other Fab Fivers—Juwan Howard, Ray Jackson, and Jimmy King. One more year to be a college kid, to play in one more Final Four and perhaps win it, to savor another year close to family, and to hone in on a degree… Webber told Wheatley those were things money could not buy.

Wheatley also wanted to set an example for his half-brother, Leslie Mongo, then 12 years old, whom he'd been a combination brother-uncle-father to while chasing his football dreams. Wheatley wanted to make a statement that education was important. Yet even with staying in school another year, Wheatley didn't earn his bachelor's degree in kinesiology from Michigan until 2008.

When we spoke in 2013, Wheatley said it was much simpler than all that. "To me," Wheatley said, "I just wasn't ready to leave Michigan. I never told anybody that. I just needed to mature."

Wheatley did not win the Heisman Trophy, as many believed he would, but he did rush for 1,144 yards and 12 touchdowns as a senior. And he still ended up being a first-round draft pick.

His days as a dazzling running back—a runaway train in cleats and shoulder pads—were over. But his success as a man of principle was only beginning. Wheatley would become Leslie's guardian; have five children with his wife, Kimberly; and settle into becoming a husband, parent, and coach.

Wheatley's own father was shot to death in the head when Tyrone was 14 months old, the victim of being in the wrong place at the wrong time during a burglary at a cousin's birthday party. His youth was filled with numerous family challenges, but he came through it all with his priorities straight. And he benefited from a number of great role models such as Michigan coach Gary Moeller, whose genuine care attracted Tyrone and pulled him away from a pre-disposition for playing at Michigan State.

"I had a conversation with Gary Moeller that took place across Schembechler Hall, which was being built, and wrapped up in his office," Wheatley said. "It made all the difference. And a lot of people don't know this—but I was not even going to take a visit to Michigan. I was going to Michigan State, Indiana, and Colorado, and I had canceled a visit to Tennessee."

But he said that Moeller, defensive coordinator Lloyd Carr, and assistant coach Jim Herrmann persisted. And finally he agreed to come on the weekend of his 19th birthday.

"It was a life conversation that I had with Gary," Wheatley said. "We talked about so much more other than football. I was a weird little cat at the time—talk to me about football and I would shut right up. He was the only coach who picked up on that. The other coaches always had their salesman's hat on. But we talked about my brother and sister, which were a focal point for me. He talked about staying close to home and representing Inkster, which was important to me. We talked about growing into a man.

"Gary Moeller is arguably the best coach I had or saw in dealing with young men, ages 17-to-22, thinking we were all Superman. But he had a way of individually getting to each player. And what I got from Michigan was the thing they preach: 'the team, the team, the team.' I was there with some incredible guys in every sport—wrestling, hockey, basketball, track, and football."

He mentioned linemen Steve Everitt, Joe Cocozzo, and Greg Skrepenak and spunky receiver Walter Smith as examples of incredible toughness and refusing to lose or even be injured.

"I had a chance to witness these guys," Wheatley said. "I learned you never, ever gave up around your teammates. It goes back to Gary Moeller and that scene from *Dead Poets Society*, where they are looking in the trophy case and learn of *carpe diem*. They are told, 'Gather ye rosebuds while ye may. Carpe diem...Seize the day!'"

That line was from a Robert Herrick poem.

"And that stuck with me," Wheatley continued. "On days when I was hurt, I looked to my right and saw Ricky Powers. I looked to my left and saw Tshimanga Biakabutuka and Jesse Johnson. If they got a chance to seize the day, they would. So I had best seize the day."

And so that is why he played hurt in the Rose Bowl and against the Buckeyes.

In March 2013, his oldest child, Tyrone Jr., received a scholarship offer from Wolverines coach Brady Hoke. He's considered a top recruit in the Class of 2015 and got his size from his mother's side of the family. Tyrone Jr. is 6'6", 235 lbs. and plays tight end and defensive end for Fayetteville-Manlius High in suburban Syracuse, New York.

"It wasn't so long ago that my sons were little boys in diapers, throwing balls around," Wheatley said. "And now my oldest son is going to get to follow his dreams. He mocks me when he sees highlights on TV about the big plays at Michigan when I was there—like Desmond [Howard] making the TD catch against Notre Dame or returning the punt for a TD against Ohio State. And even that game we lost to Colorado on the

Kordell Stewart pass. 'Where were you, Dad?' he asks. And on each one, I say, 'On the sideline.' He did not believe I played in those games, and so he mocks me."

Wheatley chuckled.

"We have fun with it," he added, "and I've told him all of my Michigan stories. But I want it to be his choice. I want my sons to realize new things and not necessarily live in my shoes."

The circle of life came around quite nicely for Tyrone Wheatley, and Superman became the family man.

CHAPTER 17

Bill McCartney and Biggie Munn

Bo Schembechler looked into Bill McCartney's eyes back in 1980 and saw a vision of Biggie Munn. Munn had coached the offensive line at Michigan under Fritz Crisler for eight seasons, and after World War II, Munn left and turned Michigan State into a national champion.

"I was asked if I was interested in the Michigan State job that Muddy Waters ended up getting," McCartney told me a few days before bringing his Colorado team to Ann Arbor in 1994. "I said, 'Sure.' A Detroit sports columnist then wrote about how Michigan State ought to go after me. Bo said they shouldn't, though, and I was happy to be where I was."

Bo forced laughter when the episode was recalled.

"Maybe I did that," he said. "Whatever I did, I did. For me, it would've been like Biggie Munn leaving Fritz Crisler and turning around Michigan State."

McCartney heeded Bo's wishes and coached two more seasons in Ann Arbor before taking over Colorado in 1982. And when he returned with the No. 7 Buffaloes to face the No. 4 Wolverines in the Big House, Bo served as the game's radio analyst on WJR-AM. He helped call a game between his most prized pupils. And it would end up being Moeller's final season at Michigan.

"It won't be weird," Bo told me at the time. "It'll be interesting to me, knowing the two staffs and how they make their moves. I'd love to see Bill win, but I hope we wax 'em."

It was classic Bo—holding out a bouquet before pulling it back in because competition outweighed compliments.

McCartney survived a 7–25–1 record his first three seasons to win the school's first national championship in 1990.

He was another Biggie Munn, all right. The Wolverines were thankful they could applaud his success from a distance. But now he was coming to town with a team that had just steamrolled defending Big Ten champion Wisconsin, 55–17.

McCartney said he was "excited to go back" to his roots with so many family and friends in attendance. But he was even more excited when the unbelievable 64-yard Hail Mary pass from Kordell Stewart to Michael Westbrook pulled out a 27–26 win.

Boulder had become home to McCartney, then 54, who was a football, basketball, and baseball star at Riverview High, not far from the Detroit River in what is known as the Downriver Area. He coached at Detroit Holy Redeemer and Dearborn Divine Child after graduating from Missouri.

However, there were always rumors that he would return to Michigan to replace Bo.

"But I always felt the job should be Gary's," McCartney said. "He didn't get a fair chance at Illinois, and I felt he was a better coach than me. I learned from him when I coached linebackers and he was defensive coordinator. I knew it was his job and never slightly pretended to be a candidate."

Bo naming Moeller at the same 1989 press conference in which he announced his retirement from coaching allowed no time for speculation.

Moeller and McCartney met on a beach in the February before they met as head coaches. They were attending a Nike convention in Hawaii but didn't talk about the game that was seven months away.

"Bill likes to walk and I like to jog, so the speeds were similar," Moeller said with some self-deprecating humor. "We had a good talk. We were good friends but not close friends.

"Every time you play a friend, though, it's special. You want to beat them because you respect them."

Both came to Bo as young men only to become their own men. Moeller was more daring with strategy; McCartney changed offensive philosophies often enough to make Bo's head spin.

Their roots were the same, though, and based on Bo's relentless work ethic and team building. "I learned a lot from Bo," McCartney said. "I'm not a fast learner, and it took me 8½ years to absorb. But the greatest lesson was a commitment to excellence."

McCartney's own touch was a commitment to Jesus Christ. He pledged the Colorado program to a verse in the Bible's book of Romans: "If the part of the dough offered as first-fruits is holy, then the whole batch is holy; if the root is holy, so are the branches."

Westbrook, one of the main heroes of that shocking 1994 win, stressed that McCartney did not overstep his bounds with his teammates.

"Coach does not preach to us unless we go in with it," Westbrook told me in a *Detroit Free Press* article during the week leading up to that game. "He lets you know it's there, and I respect him for that. He takes criticism so well and doesn't let others change him."

Dedicating his team to Christ did not keep it from encountering the problems many other major college programs have encountered. And in 1989, *Sports Illustrated* ran a "What Price Glory?" story that featured arrest-lineup photos of several of at least two dozen Buffaloes arrested between 1986 and 1989.

"I just bathed it in prayer," McCartney said. "I've made mistakes, but I always trusted the Lord to direct this program."

What many didn't realize was that Chuck Heater, then his Colorado secondary coach, was the one who invited McCartney to a meeting of Christian players at Michigan when Heater was a running back and McCartney was a new assistant on the staff.

"He committed himself to Christ then and began his walk with Him," Heater said, "and it's been an incredible walk."

After that season, McCartney felt led to focus on his Promise Keepers men's Christian fellowship group. He left coaching for good and has remained involved in various ministries. The Promise Keepers rallies packed stadiums as surely as his football teams.

Bo was proud of all the qualities and beliefs McCartney stood for. "Bill's got great resolve," Bo said then, "and I love him."

McCartney recalled the moment they parted. "Bo was the last person I saw in Ann Arbor after I cleaned out my desk," McCartney said. "He was speaking in Aspen to the Domino's Pizza board members, and we flew together to Denver.

"It was my full chance to say good-bye, to say thank you. We shook hands in the airport, and he went to his gate [for a flight to Aspen]. I went on to this job."

At Colorado, he won a national championship—something his mentor never quite accomplished. And he developed a Big Eight power house. But he only coached against Michigan one time—rather than the annual battle he would have waged with the Wolverines as the coach at Michigan State.

That could have been "Take Two" of a Bo and Woody sort of rivalry. However, McCartney would not become Munn. The family would not be broken.

CHAPTER 18

Lloyd Carr:
Staying the Course

The day you get hired for your dream job is usually a cloud-nine experience, complete with choirs of angels playing background music in the back of your mind. It is as joyous as joyous gets. And Lloyd Carr was definitely smiling on the inside the day Bo Schembechler hired him as the defensive backs coach at Michigan in 1980. But his greatest memories of that landmark day had to do with his new boss repeatedly ramming another car, telling him he was "damn dumb," and coming to Ann Arbor on a day of program scandal.

"I flew from West Virginia to Detroit for the interview with Bo," Carr said. "And when I land at Metro Airport, I pick up the *Detroit Free Press* and there is a front-page headline: 'Five Michigan Football Players Arrested on Marijuana Charges.'"

Carr shook his head at that recollection and forced a smile.

"Ann Arbor and the football offices were not an upbeat place that day," he continued. "I talked to Bo for 20 minutes to a half hour, and he asked me about my background. Lynn Koch, his secretary, came out and said, 'Bo, I've got a call for you.'"

Carr fidgeted nervously in his seat, wanting to conclude the talk and praying for a job offer.

But when Bo returned, he asked defensive coordinator Bill McCartney and assistant coach Gary Moeller, who had hired Carr at Illinois before being terminated as the head coach after three seasons, to go to lunch. McCartney grew up less than one hour's drive from Ann Arbor in Riverview, along with Carr. So Carr had some major feathers in his cap where this job was concerned.

"Bo took us all to the Pretzel Bell for lunch, and I sat up front with him in the car," Carr said. "After lunch, we go back to the parking lot and Bo backs his car out and then begins to pull forward. A guy coming down the lane just lays on his horn."

Carr paused for effect and his eyes widened.

"Bo looked in his rear-view mirror," he continued, "and Bo puts it into reverse and backs into the guy!"

Carr stopped and leaned forward, shaking his head.

"He backs into the guy to make a statement," Carr said. "And he pulls away, and this guy lays on his horn again!"

Carr leaned back and shook his head even longer. There was a look of complete disbelief in his eyes, and he sat upright before adding the zinger. "So Bo looks in the rear-view mirror one more time. And he puts it into reverse and backs into the guy again!

"Bo waits a few seconds to check the rear-view mirror. And this time, the guy is gone," Carr chuckled.

The horn-honker had no idea that the vengeful driver with a demolition driver's bent was Bo the Terrible. He simply put it in reverse and ran for cover.

"No," Carr said, "there wasn't even any damage to the cars somehow. It was just bumper on bumper."

They made it back to the football offices at the corner of State and Hoover without further incident, and Carr walked down the hall with Bo to continue the interview.

Carr recalled, "Bo said, 'You'd kind of like to work here, wouldn't you?' And I quickly answered, 'Yes, sir.' Then Lynn Koch comes to the door again and tells Bo he has another call. This was a crazy day. Bo says, 'Excuse me.' So I go into the room where Lynn and Mary Passink [also a football coach secretary] are.

"McCartney comes in and says, 'Lloyd, did he hire you?' I said, 'I don't know.' Now, three or four minutes pass and Bo comes back. McCartney says, 'Bo, did you hire him?'

"Bo got an incredulous look on his face and said, 'Well, didn't he tell you?'

"McCartney shrugged his shoulders and responded, 'He said he didn't know, Bo.'

"Bo took the incredulousness up a couple notches and bellowed, 'If he's too damn dumb to know I hired him, then he's too damn dumb to work here.'"

End of topic, end of conversation, end of the drama.

A smile creased Carr's face and he added, "That's how I got hired."

So much for warm fuzzies or any sort of motivational speech about joining the coaching staff and helping "the team, the team, the team" win a Big Ten championship. However, the Wolverines did win the conference title and Bo's first Rose Bowl in that 1980 season.

Carr had found his permanent home and would help coach Michigan to 13 Big Ten championships.

He'd just completed the most transient point in his career—getting fired along with Moeller at Illinois; getting hired at West Virginia by another former Bo assistant, Don Nehlen; and then joining the Michigan staff all in a period of less than four months.

"Me and Mo moved into the Lamplighter Hotel for a couple months and got going on the job," Carr said.

For all the anxiety Carr experienced the day he got the job, March 12, 1980, he had a pretty good idea about landing it even before leaving Morgantown, West Virginia.

"I had a recruit with me and took him back to meet Coach Nehlen," Carr said. "He said, 'Lloyd, I just had a call from Bo Schembechler. He wants to talk to you.' Then he looked me in the eye and said, 'You need to get up early and take all of your stuff with you. Bo's going to hire you.'"

Nehlen knew Bo well enough to believe that he was more than a little interested in Carr, who would coach at Michigan for the next 28 years and spend the final 13 as the head coach.

However, Carr could very well have left after one year as the head coach. He was given the interim tag on May 15, 1995, after Moeller was forced out as the head coach. Wolverines athletic director Joe Roberson, upon the announcement, said Carr "would not be the head coach other than on an interim basis" and tabled the hiring of the program's next head coach.

Roberson consulted those he valued both inside and outside the program, and Penn State coach Joe Paterno, the legendary leader of the newest member of the Big Ten, was one person Roberson particularly sought out for insight.

"I leaned on Joe Paterno," Roberson said. "Joe told me, 'You can hire any coach you want right now, but think of the ramifications of the timing. Think of the ethics of doing that at this time of the year. You would be uprooting coaches and assistant coaches from their kids.' Joe told me, 'Why not make Lloyd your interim coach and take it from there?' And that made perfect sense."

Though, contacting Paterno, for whom Bo had supreme respect, rubbed the former Wolverines coach and athletic director the wrong way.

"I caught hell from Bo for doing that, talking to Joe," Roberson said. "You weren't supposed to talk to anybody but Bo."

In Carr's first game that August, Michigan overcame a 17–0 deficit to beat Virginia 18–17. The Wolverines were off to a 5–0 start with the largest comeback victory in school history. Scott Dreisbach's 15-yard touchdown pass to Mercury Hayes in the right corner of the end zone on the final play of that Pigskin Classic game did more than give Michigan a big win—it gave Carr some much-needed momentum as a head coaching possibility.

Carr's popularity rose as surely as the team's rank in the Associated Press poll during that winning streak when the Wolverines went from

No. 14 to No. 6 in the country. The players clearly enjoyed playing for Carr, who was getting results. He also brought a constancy and sense of tradition that an outsider could not touch. It still felt, sounded, and smelled like Big House football to the school's Old Blues.

Roberson said he had been sold on Carr from the beginning, but Roberson had some convincing to do with Michigan president James Duderstadt and other top school administrators.

"I am not sure that Lloyd got the job with the blessings of everyone," Roberson said. "There were still people critical of the hire at the time I made it. Early on, I had a meeting with the top three authority figures at the school. And after our conversation, I was the only one who wanted Lloyd.

Coach Lloyd Carr (right) high fives Chad Henne after the quarterback threw a touchdown pass in the second quarter against Notre Dame in South Bend, Indiana, on September 16, 2006. (AP Photo/Joe Raymond)

"But Jim [Duderstadt] came to like the choice of Lloyd for two reasons. First, Jim realized any appointment from outside the Michigan staff was a risk. Second, Jim traveled with the team that year on trips. He began to feel a higher level of respect for Lloyd on the trips."

Carr was elevated to full-time head coach on November 13, 1995, with an 8–2 record after beating Purdue and Mike Alstott 5–0 on an icy Michigan Stadium field that seemed more like the surface Coach Red Berenson's team played on at Yost Ice Arena.

However, there were politics being played that entire season, and the behind-the-scenes mind games and power plays nearly caused Carr to turn down the job. The cost of becoming the long-term head coach, surprisingly, appeared to be way too high. At one juncture the job would come only with Carr's conditional denouncing of Bo, which would have meant becoming a football coaching Judas. And the message with that request was delivered by something of a "Deep Throat" character who Carr wished to keep anonymous even to this day.

"Somebody came up to my office, an authority figure in the athletic department," Carr said. "He said it came from the highest authority at the University of Michigan. He said, 'If you want to be the head coach at Michigan, you should divorce or separate yourself from Bo.' But I thought, *If that's what it takes to get that job, I don't want it.*"

Duderstadt, who held the highest post at the school from 1988 until July 1996, once told me that college athletics had become too big and that having network television and the rising power of ESPN controling football and basketball was wrong. If he had his way, athletic scholarships would have been done away with and intercollegiate sports would resemble intramurals more than another version of professional sports.

Yet Duderstadt realized that was not realistic. The horse was out of the barn, and it was too late for that kind of massive reform. He also knew that there was very little support among his colleagues for the toning down of high-profile collegiate athletics. For better or worse, sports programs have become the most visible images of major universities. There are large numbers of desirable high school applicants who make Wolverines football and basketball strong considerations in choosing Michigan over Ivy League schools, and many of the biggest financial donors to the university are also huge athletic department boosters.

But that didn't mean Duderstadt had to enjoy viewing that landscape, and he clearly did not. Duderstadt saw Bo as the epitome of college athletics wielding too much power on campus and loathed him.

"They did not want Bo to become the A.D.," Carr said. "It was a political war. Bo won the war, and they had not forgotten that."

Bo became the athletic director the same year Duderstadt became president, and they co-existed for two years before Bo left to become president of the Detroit Tigers for Tom Monaghan, his friend and a Wolverines booster.

But before departing, Bo named Moeller his successor with no search committee, no discussion. That angered some in the school's administration, but it was Bo's program and he would run it the way he saw fit.

Roberson said he was not aware of the conversation Carr had with an athletic department "authority figure," but he did not discredit Carr's account of having to denounce Bo to get the job. What did happen was that Carr won out over Duderstadt. Carr had qualities that most of his predecessors and successors at Michigan did not. If ever there was a Renaissance man in charge of the Wolverines, it was Carr.

"I was never worried about Lloyd having success as a coach," Roberson said, "but he also had other qualities I knew about that would make him a true role model to his players. That appealed to me. We traded books, and there was an intellectual side to Lloyd. I would go into Lloyd's office and hear classical music. You don't hear that very often in football offices."

Roberson touched on Carr using *Into Thin Air* by Jon Krakauer as a motivational theme for the 1997 season, which ended with the Wolverines symbolically climbing their own Mount Everest. The Krakauer book dealt with a Mount Everest disaster during which eight climbers were killed and several were stranded by a surprise storm.

"Lloyd gave each player on the team a pickaxe as a symbol that year so they knew they were in the climb together, and he quoted *Into Thin Air* during the season," Roberson said.

Quarterback Brian Griese laughed about the potential for disaster in giving a whole team of football players Maize and Blue pickaxes, but nobody gouged an eye out.

And in the Rose Bowl locker room after beating Washington State to finish an undefeated national championship season, Carr proclaimed, "We went to the summit—we're there!"

Carr often found encouragement and messages in literature for his team. Roberson pointed to the words of Rudyard Kipling's "The Law of the Jungle" poem from *The Jungle Book* that Carr had painted onto a football team meeting room:

"For the strength of the Pack is the Wolf,
"And the strength of the Wolf is the Pack."

And for a team nicknamed the Wolverines, what could be a better bonding statement? "A whole lot of football coaches think Rudyard Kipling is a middle linebacker at Alcorn State," Roberson said. "But Lloyd knows so much about literature, music, and life."

Mostly, he knew how to get through to people. "He communicates so well with the kids," Moeller told me. "And Lloyd had a great way of always doing what needed to be done. He knew his football, too. But the main thing you have to do as a coach is getting them to play mentally, and Lloyd had that down."

Oddly enough, Carr nearly became an assistant coach at arch-rival Michigan State with George Perles. But the Spartans passed over Perles at that time for Muddy Waters, hiring Perles three years later as Waters' replacement. Perles offered Carr a chance to be his defensive coordinator at MSU in 1983, but Carr declined after Bo assured him he would eventually become his defensive coordinator.

"I was honored that George asked me to join him in those jobs," Carr said, "and I liked George a lot. But I knew I was going to be the defensive coordinator at Michigan in time and just loved it there."

Carr was elevated to that position in 1987 when Moeller moved out of that role and became the offensive coordinator.

Notre Dame Coach Lou Holtz and Pittsburgh Steelers Coach Chuck Noll also made offers, but Carr never left Michigan. He coached the defensive backs, coordinated the defense, and became the head coach of the Wolverines. Carr coached 28 seasons in the Big House, spending seven more years there than Bo himself. Only Bennie Oosterbaan, who came as an assistant in 1928 and was a head coach for 11 seasons before retiring in 1958, coached longer on a Michigan staff with his 31 seasons.

And Carr's finest job of coaching might have come in a game from 1997 that is often forgotten in light of the Penn State dismantling, classic victory over Ohio State, and the Rose Bowl win over Washington State that season. The dream season very well could have come apart on October 18 in Ann Arbor when No. 15 Iowa took it to the Wolverines in the first half and grabbed a 21–7 lead.

"That might very well have been the biggest coaching job Lloyd did that whole season," said Mike DeBord, who was in his first season as the offensive coordinator. "I thought he would let loose on the players in the locker room at half time, but he didn't.

"Instead, Lloyd stood there and asked, 'Is there any man here who does not believe we're the better team?'"

The players immediately and quite vocally affirmed their belief that they were superior to Iowa. Carr continued, "Then let's go out there and play Michigan football and win this game. And do it one play at a time." He then instructed the players to get with their position coaches and make the necessary adjustments in the second half.

DeBord added, "That was the big turning point in that season. We'd never played that poorly and hadn't been behind by much. It wasn't us.

But he regrouped that whole team."

Griese threw three interceptions in that game, but in the second half he ran for a touchdown on fourth-and-goal at the 1 and threw his third touchdown pass with 2:55 remaining. Griese scrambled and found tight end Jerame Tuman for the two-yard touchdown that put the Wolverines up 28–24. Linebacker Sam Sword sealed the victory by intercepting Hawkeyes quarterback Matt Sherman at the Michigan 15-yard line with 31 seconds left.

"We scored that touchdown at the end, and the defense secured it," DeBord said. "We beat Iowa, and if we had not, we would not have won a national championship." And it was the first Michigan national championship since 1948 when Oosterbaan was in his first year as head coach after succeeding his longtime mentor Fritz Crisler.

Seldom does assistant coaching loyalty translate into such advancement followed by such success. But it worked for Carr, who began his path to major college football along with two of his friends from Riverview High who went on to become football coaching forces, too. The journey began with McCartney and Woody Widenhofer in a blue-collar town along the Detroit River where Carr's photo still hangs at the school and a city park is named for him.

McCartney—best known as the head coach of a blockbuster program at the University of Colorado where he won a national championship in 1990—was the only high school coach Bo ever hired after McCartney's ultra-successful stint as the head coach at Dearborn (Michigan) Divine Child High. Carr followed McCartney's lead by also electing to play for Dan Devine at the University of Missouri, just as Widenhofer did. However, Carr would transfer to Northern Michigan as a senior in 1967 and quarterback the Wildcats to an undefeated season before graduating with an education degree at the Upper Peninsula university. Carr followed McCartney once again 13 years later, getting the Michigan job.

Widenhofer, however, nearly pried Carr away from the home he'd found in Ann Arbor. In 1983, just after Carr decided against taking the defensive coordinator's post in East Lansing, Widenhofer called from Pittsburgh with an offer to interview for the linebacker coach position. Widenhofer was the defensive coordinator for the Steelers and their legendary head coach, Chuck Noll, and had helped mold the famed Steel Curtain defense that won four Super Bowls in the 1970s.

It was a chance to join another dynasty. And Carr was familiar with Noll, too, after several visits to Pittsburgh's training camps in Latrobe, Pennsylvania, where Carr would observe and absorb coaching points that would be used with the Wolverines.

"Woody called and said, 'You need to come in for an interview,'" Carr said. "I said, 'Woody, I can't.'"

Having just received the assurances about his future from Bo and knowing the summer was "bad timing" for a coaching departure, Carr declined the interview. However, Widenhofer persisted and Carr received another surprising call from his longtime friend.

"I talked to Chuck," Widenhofer told Carr, "and the job is yours."

Carr was taken aback, and he decided to call Bo and inform him of the offer.

"Bo told me to hold on and that he was coming over to my house," Carr said. "It was the only time I can remember that he did that.

"Bo came in and looked at me, and crinkled up his eyes the way he did. And then he said, 'You're not a pro coach! You're a college coach. You should be working with kids. That's a business in the NFL. This is about making an impact on kids' lives!'"

And so Carr stayed and thrived not only as a coach but as a teacher and mentor. He shared books and thoughts with players and remained in their lives years after they left Michigan.

Carr chuckled, also recalling the overtures from Lou Holtz and Notre Dame in 1990.

"Bo said, 'You aren't going there! You're Michigan!'"

Carr stopped to reflect on how resisting temptations and heeding Bo's advice paid off. It probably made sense to join Holtz in South Bend because Moeller was becoming Michigan's head coach, and Carr very well could have succeeded Holtz when he walked away from Notre Dame after the 1996 season. But he ended up taking over at Michigan in that tumultuous 1995 season and winning a national championship in his third season as head coach. And he stayed 13 seasons as the head coach, riding off into the sunset on the shoulder pads of his players after winning his final bowl game.

"Bo made it clear to me in a very concise manner," said Carr, his voice beginning to crack. He paused and quickly glanced to his right and left. Then Carr looked up, his eyes reflecting pure passion, and he shook his head while soaking in the significance of the path he chose to take.

Carr smiled slowly and said, "Look at what happened to me. None of what happened to me would have happened if I hadn't listened. No, none of it."

CHAPTER 19

Friday Night Lights in the Big House

When Lloyd Carr took over as the head coach at Michigan, he was prompted to begin a preseason tradition that was his version of campfire tales for football players. It was based on a comment he once read from announcer Keith Jackson, who was what college football would sound like if it had a voice.

Carr said, "What Keith said was this: 'Tradition in college football is Michigan Stadium on the Friday night before a game.'"

Fans in town for Saturday's game often drift over to the Big House after dinner at the Gandy Dancer, Real Seafood Company, or the classic Fleetwood Diner. They walk into its open gates and sit in the stands or walk on the field. They feel the ghosts of Tom Harmon and Bo Schembechler. They point to the north end zone to tell their children that "there—right there" Desmond Howard stretched out like a slinky to catch a touchdown pass from Elvis Grbac to beat Notre Dame.

They soak up the past and pass it on to their children or grandchildren.

It is a shrine to anyone wearing the Maize and Blue as much as it is a stadium. It has changed much since Fielding H. Yost authorized the digging of a big hole in the ground at the corner of Main Street and Stadium Boulevard, and it now has a towering press box on the west side and an equally majestic span of luxury boxes on the east side. But what happens on the 100 yards below has never varied, and some of the sport's greatest games, in what is approaching a full century of kickoffs,

169

An aerial view of Michigan Stadium is seen from the Spirit of Goodyear airship on Friday, August 15, 2008, in Ann Arbor, Michigan. A three-year, $226 million project added 82 luxury suites, a new press box, improved stadium seating, and concourse fan amenities to the Big House.
(AP Photo/Tony Ding)

have been played there.

Carr never wanted his players to take for granted the place where they played, so he had an idea.

"On the last day of training camp, before we go into a regular week of practice preparation for the first game," Carr said, "I would take the entire team up to the stadium that Friday night. I did that with every team that I coached.

"I would get them all gathered around in a big circle and say, 'This is our stadium this year. We get these six or seven games here, and that's it. You will have the memories of these games your whole life.'"

Jim Schneider, a retired Michigan sports information department publicist who worked closely with Carr, Gary Moeller, and Bo, smiled while listening to Carr recall the scene of those bonding expeditions at the stadium.

"We didn't have lights then," Schneider said. "It was dark, and the only light would come from the few lights in the tunnel or the moon."

If they ever make a movie about Charles Woodson, Brian Griese, and the 1997 national champions, recalling their Friday night from that season on film would be a must.

"We would all circle on the field," Carr said, "and I would have the captains talk. And they often said the same kinds of things they had heard when they first came to the team: You have to say to yourself, 'Every day that I am going to be here, I am going to do my best every one of those days. And for you freshmen, you have so much to learn on how to be a real part of a team. Listening will be most important for you.'

"And then other players would chip in and say things that were on their minds. I did it every year for 13 years. It was a fun thing, a great night."

Carr leaned back with the satisfied look of an old coach who knew how to bring together some 100 players from across the country, from entirely different lifestyles and even different languages, at the start of a new campaign through the Big Ten.

"When I got to introduce and speak about Brian Griese at the Rose Bowl Hall of Fame induction," Carr said of the December 2012 event, "I went out to eat with Keith Jackson and Bob Griese. And at that dinner, we talked about that."

For each of them, and for so many fans of the Wolverines, there is much more to it than what is visible on football Saturdays. There is that special matter of football Fridays without the lights.

CHAPTER 20

Tshimanga Biakabutuka:
The All-Time Diamond in the Rough

Michigan's greatest single-season rusher was one of the most unlikely heroes in school history. If you had created him as a character in a fictional Chip Hilton–type sports novel, publishers would have rejected it as too far-fetched.

A great running back from Africa would be wild enough. But then to have him move to Montreal and become a football star in Canada before getting a scholarship to Michigan…well, that's just not plausible. But it happened.

Tshimanga "Tim" Biakabutuka was born in Kinshasa, Zaire, and raised outside of Montreal. He was off the map as far as recruiting services were concerned, but he fell into Michigan's lap and put together one of the school's most memorable games and seasons.

In 1995, Biakabutuka ran for 194 yards or more in four games. His 313 yards against Ohio State sparked an upset win over Ohio State and upstaged Eddie George, the Buckeyes' Heisman Trophy winner that year. Biakabutuka broke Jamie Morris' rushing record with 1,818 yards on the season and left after his junior year to become a first-round pick of the Carolina Panthers.

Tyrone Wheatley, perhaps the best running back in school history and Biakabutuka's teammate, told me a story that put the deceptiveness of Biakabutuka's cuts into perspective.

"Everybody jokes about a move that tore a guy's ACL or caused him to leave his jock strap on the ground," Wheatley said. "Well, in a spring practice, Biakabutuka put a move on [inside linebacker] Rob Swett that was so hard that he tore his ACL. He puts a move on a cat that is so hard that he tears his ACL!"

As that 1995 season wound down, the *Detroit Free Press* sent me to his hometown of Longueuil, Quebec, to chronicle his story. I drove from Montreal across the St. Lawrence River to the family home and knocked on the front door. His mother, Misenga Batuabile Bibi, opened the door and I walked into a living room decorated with Biakabutuka's trophies and posters.

Misenga said she couldn't fathom the importance of football in the United States or the fame and free college education it has brought her son. And now two of her younger sons—Beya and Joseph Biakabutuka—were playing football, too, and gaining attention from colleges.

Beya was attending Vanier College, the same prep school Tshimanga went to.

"I want to do like my brother," Beya said. "He is my example to follow."

And the Biakabutukas are faithful in following their convictions, some of them deeply religious.

"We have done well with our children, with God's help," Misenga said.

Tshimanga would run over the Buckeyes later that week, but neither of his parents would be in the Big House. His father, Mulenga Wa Biakabutuka, was fulfilling his duties as a teacher at a Cree Indian reservation on the banks of the Waswanipi River. Mulenga made the nine-hour drive from lumberjack country in a forgotten corner of Quebec to his home as often as he could, but that was not often.

Misenga, a clothing designer, had gone to Zaire the previous week to sell clothes at a reduced cost in their homeland. The Biakabutukas moved to Canada from Zaire in 1980 when Mulenga went to study at the University of Montreal.

"She is trying to help the people back there," Tshimanga told me upon my return. "There is a lot of political unrest, and I did not want her to go. There are no phones for us to talk, and she stays a month. But she will do what she does."

The Biakabutukas have a dozen children—six boys and six girls with 26 years between the youngest and oldest. The three oldest girls remained in Kinshasa.

Tshimanga (pronounced tuh-MONG-ah) speaks Tshiluba, one of the two African dialects he knows, when speaking to his mother. Biakabutuka (bee-OCK-ah-buh-too-kuh) translates to "born again" in that language.

And in the second of three countries Biakabutuka would call home, speaking the second of three languages he mastered, he became a trailblazer. "Tshimanga is the first French-speaking football player who has made it big in American college football," said Jean-Charles Meffe, then the technical director for Football Quebec, which oversees the sport at all levels in the province.

"Now football is quite popular. It shows our kids you can become somebody with this sport, and he is responsible for that. Thirteen schools have added varsity football in the Montreal area just this year."

All of this was somewhat overwhelming for the player who was often called Touchdown Tim at Michigan. "I have a big responsibility in Quebec," Biakabutuka said. "I can't get arrested or do something silly here, and I must get my degree—my mother reminds me that is the reason I am here. Maybe I have had a good influence, so football took another step there. Kids can see me on TV and hope for a scholarship."

Serge Benoit, his coach at Jacques Rousseau High in Montreal, discovered Biakabutuka when he was 15. "I noticed his athletic ability," Benoit said, "and asked, 'Why don't you play football?' He looked at me and said, 'If I play, I want to go far.' He was an aggressive character but easy to coach.

"After three practices, I could see he was special. He could change speeds easily and made good decisions because of his great vision of the field. And then he had success and did not think of himself as something special. He never missed a practice."

Biakabutuka went from high school to CEGEP, the Quebec college prep program, and picked Vanier. Vieux Montreal was closer to home and had the superior athletics department, but Vanier had a better academic reputation. So he made the 75-minute commute twice daily on the Metro bus system.

"Tshimanga was a walk-on, and we did not recruit him," former Vanier coach Tim Matuzewski said. "He was such a diamond in the rough, but in 13 years of coaching I have never seen another kid like him in this area.

"Tshimanga had the ability to turn every play into a touchdown and keep the fans on the edge of their seats."

However, Biakabutuka's story might never have included wearing a Maize and Blue winged helmet. If Vieux Montreal coach Marc Santerre had not taken Biakabutuka and several other area prospects to Michigan's summer football camp in 1992, he never would've showed up on Coach Gary Moeller's radar.

The Wolverines couldn't believe the raw talent that had been dropped into their laps and that they had a player for which the term "diamond in the rough" was insufficient.

Given the chance, Biakabutuka went from a long-shot to a game-changer. He was not as highly recruited as many of the Wolverines he competed against for playing time—Tyrone Wheatley and Ed Davis— but he had a drive fueled by relatives remaining in Africa.

"I have a lot of cousins in Africa who do not have the chance to do something with their lives," Biakabutuka said. "When I'm tired and beat up, I think of them. They would do anything to have this chance.

"And my parents helped a lot, too. Mom said to respect others, and if you respect, you stay humble. You strive to get better if you're humble because you never feel you're too good. Dad says to be strong and believe you can do whatever anybody can."

His dad drove nine hours to work. His mom flew to Africa to transport clothes. So what is 100 yards to cross?

Biakabutuka had a perspective few college football stars could understand.

"A lot of people back home laughed when I did not play much my first year at Michigan," Biakabutuka said of the 1993 season when he had 43 carries for 209 yards. "But I knew after my first scrimmage that I could play here. So I lifted and ran and put so much into making it.

"People say I could win the Heisman Trophy next year, and that is nice. But why do you need somebody to tell you how good you are with an award? If I feel in my heart I am the best in the nation, I've accomplished my goals."

Lloyd Carr, who would coach Michigan in 1995, said Biakabutuka would've been the Heisman front-runner that year. And Biakabutuka thought he would be back until the Ohio State game, the runaway train game, vaulted him into the Top 10 players available in the NFL draft.

And for what it was worth—and in this case it might have been literally a few million dollars—Biakabutuka was taken ahead of OSU's Eddie George. Biakabutuka was taken eighth overall, and the Houston Oilers took George with the 16th pick.

Biakabutuka signed a six-year, $12.5 million contract with the Carolina Panthers. Injuries plagued him, however, and then claimed him.

On October 21, 2001, on an afternoon when Biakabutuka rushed for one touchdown and a career-high 121 yards at Washington's FedEx Field, he was gang-tackled and had his right foot mangled on what would be the final play of his football career. And just like that, his best day became his worst day.

Pain rushed up his right leg as the tendons in the foot tore apart, leaving his foot dangling. There was an initial fear that amputation might be required without immediate surgery.

The foot was saved, but Biakabutuka knew his career could not be salvaged. The foot stability required to make cuts on a dime was lost. He started for two seasons, rushing for a career-high 718 yards and six touchdowns in 1999. But he had just four 100-yard rushing games in the NFL and never attained greatness as a pro.

Biakabutuka sought to find his niche as a businessman, and he finally found it in 2007 as the president and owner of Beya Jewelry in Charlotte. It was named for his grandfather and brother, and Biakabutuka sold inventory that included a Christian-themed line of gold and diamond jewelry that he designed.

Panthers owner Jerry Richardson mentored and advised him in business, and one of his investors was Muhsin Muhammad, who played against Biakabutuka at Michigan State and then with him on the Panthers.

Now he owns three Bojangles' Famous Chicken 'n Biscuits restaurants in and near Augusta, Georgia. And so the kid from Canada by way of Africa who became a football star in Ann Arbor before becoming an NFL first-round pick now lives in a town where golf's hallowed Masters Tournament is played and has become Mr. Bojangles.

The only thing predictable about Tshimanga Biakabutuka is that he's been unpredictable at nearly every turn.

CHAPTER 21

Brian Griese and Growing Up

There were dozens of talented football players who blossomed to bring Michigan its national championship in 1997. That's how it goes with great teams. An amazing number of players all peaked in that same wonderful year.

Brian Griese was one of those players, but to me he was the one who most symbolizes that team. Griese had been mediocre until that season, and the Wolverines had become mediocre. They were coming off four consecutive four-loss seasons and had not finished higher than third in the Big Ten in any of them.

The four-year seniors from 1996 became the first players since Bo Schembechler's arrival in 1969 to leave Ann Arbor without a Big Ten championship. Bo had promised that "Those Who Stay Will Be Champions," but that class did not become champions. And it included three tough-as-nails All-Americans: defensive tackle William Carr, linebacker Jarrett Irons, and center Rod Payne.

Griese came to Michigan with them in the fall of 1993 and was redshirted as a walk-on. Had he played that year, then he, too, would've been elsewhere in 1997. He would have missed his date with destiny.

And there's a good chance Griese would not have even been drafted without that golden year. He had thrown for just 513 yards with three touchdowns and two interceptions as a junior in 1996 when he backed up Scott Dreisbach.

Griese was a talented high school quarterback at Christopher Columbus High in Miami, where his father, Bob, was a Hall of Fame quarterback for the Miami Dolphins. Brian had some pretty good scholarship offers from major college programs.

However, Brian wanted to go to school at Michigan. And, along with his father, he believed quarterbacks coach Cam Cameron would help him develop. Bob could afford to pay for his son to attend an expensive out-of-state school. And so they rolled the dice and Brian went to Ann Arbor.

Griese held on place-kicks in 1994 and saw his only significant action just before his senior year in 1995. Dreisbach was injured in the fifth game that year, and Griese came on to throw for 1,577 yards with 13 touchdowns and 10 interceptions. He was far from fabulous, however, and got crushed by Texas A&M in the Alamo Bowl. Some observers lost faith in his ability to be something special on a football field. But he really had no chance to excel in that bowl game. The Aggies cut through the Wolverines' offensive line like a hot knife through butter, and Griese had few opportunities to go through progressions with his receivers. He was too busy running for his life.

And then there was the incident at the Scorekeepers sports bar in Ann Arbor. Griese insisted on using the emergency exit to the alley and set off alarms in doing so. Eventually, he was told to leave. Upon exiting the front door, Griese angrily shattered the large window at the entry. He was arrested, and Lloyd Carr fumed. He had not been happy with Griese for other reasons, and now Carr was livid.

"He made a mistake," Carr said. "He paid for it."

He put Griese on an extremely tight and short leash. One more miscue and Griese could have been gone. But that was his last source of embarrassment in Ann Arbor. He did what plenty of kids do when they go away to college. He grew up, took responsibility for himself, and became all he could be as a senior.

But Griese did make one mistake in judgment prior to his senior season. Carr said Griese told *Detroit News* reporter Angelique Chengelis that he would "need some assurances" in order to return for 1997 as a fifth-year senior. Carr had Griese summoned to his office immediately.

"Brian comes in, and I am mad," Carr said. "I told him that I had read his comments and repeated them to him. He said, 'Yeah, I said that.' So I had this response for Brian. 'This is the only assurance you will get from me. I will give you an opportunity to win the job—no assurances.' He was good with that.

"And all spring and all summer he was working as hard as he could. He got into the best shape of his life; he matured, grew up. He was everything you wanted."

Carr was so impressed that he even decided to give him that assurance he'd wanted before earning it.

"I called him into my office that July," Carr said, "and I said, 'Look, the job is yours. You earned it.' I wanted him to know I had confidence in him. I wanted him to be a leader."

It's funny how things work out sometimes. A coach has a player who makes him want to pull out his hair, and wonders what the future holds. Will he ever grow up? And then, in the stretch run, he does.

There are more stories of talent never realized than most fans realize. For every blue-chip recruit who becomes a star and moves on to professional football, there is one who either doesn't play much or doesn't start until he's a senior, then there is another who transfers, and there is one who drops out.

About 25 players a year come to Ann Arbor with dreams of greatness. Most are red-shirted and a few play their first four years and leave. So there are usually more than 100 players on the roster every year. There are 22 starters. You do the math.

But Griese didn't become a casualty. He became the Most Valuable Player of the Rose Bowl win that capped a season so good that even Griese himself could not have seen it coming—not in his wildest dreams.

He threw for 2,293 yards and 17 touchdowns as a senior, was named

All-Big Ten first-team, and threw for 251 yards and three touchdowns against Washington State in the 21–16 Rose Bowl victory in Pasadena that capped a 12–0 season. He joined his father, who won with Purdue on January 1, 1967, as a Rose Bowl Most Valuable Player.

Bob Griese did a great job that week and during that game of being both a dad and Keith Jackson's broadcast partner on ABC-TV. That's a difficult thing to do—being objective about the son you photographed kneeling on the Rose Bowl logo at midfield days before the game.

But his son took Bob off the hook by stealing the show. There was little criticism needed by the network analyst.

When it came time to announce the MVP, Jackson, in that certain-yet-folksy manner of his, said, "The MVP—I'm standing beside his proud Daddy.... Go ahead and cry."

And the Daddy's eyes welled up with tears.

"I've done well all year," said the father, who usually insisted on calling his youngest son "Griese" while discussing the Michigan quarterback on telecasts. "...But, well, it was special."

Brian's take on his dad's sentiments: "That's not my dad." Loving Bob was, but emotional he generally was not.

Fans watched that scene unfold while viewing the game with family and friends on New Year's Day. They might not have known a thing about football, but they knew that what they were watching was indeed something "special," something that made every son think of his father and every father think of his son.

And when Brian joined his father in the Rose Bowl Hall of Fame in 2012, he thanked the two men most responsible for his success. Brian went back to Pasadena 15 years after his triumph and four years after his NFL career ended. He rode in the Tournament of Roses Parade in a convertible and waved to the fans along Colorado Boulevard. At his induction speech, Brian Griese thanked his father and Lloyd Carr.

"I introduced Brian before he gave his acceptance speech in Pasadena," Carr said. "And that speech he gave.... It was something."

Brian Griese and Growing Up

Quarterback and game MVP Brian Griese leaves the field accompanied by Wolverines fans after the 84th Rose Bowl in Pasadena, California, on Thursday, January 1, 1998. Michigan beat Washington State 21-16. (AP Photo/Reed Saxon)

It's funny how things work out sometimes.

A player thinks his coach and the whole world are out to get him one day. He wonders why he ever chose to come to Ann Arbor and experience one frustration after another. And then one day he realizes it was all part of the process, part of his growth. He realizes that one of those sayings coaches like telling players—what doesn't break you makes you stronger—really was true. Players think their coaches are corny with such clichés because the players are, after all, invincible. But then they get knocked down and are handed a challenge. Their invincibility does not come to the rescue. And they find that the only way to survive and thrive is to dig deeper than they ever have before.

Griese understands all of that now.

And as proud as he is of his college career and becoming a Pro Bowl quarterback and Super Bowl champion with the Denver Broncos, he also came to realize that the game was just a game. It was what the game could allow you to do off the field that really mattered most in the big picture. Baubles and trophies are fun for a while, but Judi's House is about forever.

Brian opened Judi's House, which he built in Denver and put into operation to serve as a center of grief support and belonging for children dealing with the death and illness of a parent, in honor of his mother, who died of cancer when he was 10.

Griese also made a significant donation and gave his time to Mott Children's Hospital in Ann Arbor where former Wolverines teammates Charles Woodson and Steve Hutchinson also made their mark by following the lead of Carr and putting their imprint on something larger than a football field. There was a girl in that hospital with an illness when Griese played at Michigan. She wrote him letters, and he wrote back. He even took her to the prom.

Griese made his name in football but also made his mark by comforting others. He not only symbolized a team that overcame mediocrity but a team that touched hearts.

CHAPTER 22

A Coach Savors the 1997 National Championship

How do you savor a national championship?

A) You raise a toast and smoke a cigar with your mentor.

B) You take a long morning walk down memory lane in Pasadena.

C) You watch a player jump for joy before getting his ring.

D) All of the above.

If you are Lloyd Carr, you cherished it by doing all of the above.

After beating Washington State 21–16 in the Rose Bowl, the Wolverines had no idea that they would split the 1997 national championship with Nebraska. But they knew they were 12–0, and that was something to celebrate.

Upon returning to his suite at the Double Tree Hotel in downtown Pasadena, Carr had a message requesting him to join Bo Schembechler and his party at the hotel's bar and grill.

"I get there and Bo and a bunch of former players are smoking cigars," Carr said. "Well, there was one problem. California had just implemented a new non-smoking ordinance on January 1. But they were drinking and smoking and having a great time.

"The hotel informed them of the new ordinance, but they didn't care. So, they called the police on them. They were kind of nervous about confronting a bunch of 270-lb. football players, but they did. But those guys said, 'We just won the national championship. We're going to smoke

Head coach Lloyd Carr watches his players practice on December 26, 1997, at Citrus College in Glendora, California, in preparation for the Rose Bowl game on January 1, 1998. (AP Photo/Chris Urso)

these cigars!' So they kicked them out! The police ruined our party at the Double Tree that night."

While exiting the area, Carr ran into tight end Mark Campbell.

Carr said, "Mark Campbell said, 'Coach, you've been drinking!' I said, 'Campbell, I have not been drinking. Don't you ever say that again!'"

Carr, who admitted to having "had a couple beers," laughed after recalling the story.

If only Campbell had known that the police had been called in to break up the party. He could have had Carr run stair laps next year with that kind of information. But it was definitely a night to remember for the celebrations that popped up in Pasadena and anywhere groups of happy revelers wearing Maize and Blue gathered.

Carr awoke the next morning at 5:00 AM and opted to go for a long walk. There was a light rain, and the sun had yet to rise. But there was someplace he felt the need to visit. "I walked from the Double Tree to the Ritz-Carlton, which had been the Sheraton in the old days," Carr said. "It was a beautiful time for me, that walk was. I thought back to staying there when we won Bo's first Rose Bowl in my first year coaching on his staff [in 1981]. And what a beautiful, happy time that was. I walked around the lobby and reminisced.

"And I thought of something Keith Jackson once told me of how all the other conferences were always jealous of the Big Ten and the Pac-10 having the Rose Bowl locked up. Everything about it, the whole experience was special—just so special."

That night, No. 2 Nebraska put a 42–17 shellacking on No. 3 Tennessee in the Orange Bowl. And when the final polls were released on January 3, Michigan remained No. 1 in the Associated Press poll and claimed half of the national championship. Nebraska, after going 13–0 with the extra win coming in the Big 12 championship game, jumped ahead of the Wolverines to finish No. 1 and claim the crown in the *USA Today*/ESPN poll voted upon by coaches.

Some were upset about having to share a national title with the

Cornhuskers, but nobody was complaining on that day in the spring when the national championship rings were presented before the senior class departed.

"We handed out the rings in late April in the team meeting room," Carr said. "I opened the door to come into the room and will not forget that scene as long as I live.

"They were bringing in a cart with the rings on it right behind me. They were all seated there, and I spotted [linebacker] Ian Gold on the edge of one row. Ian turns around and sees the rings. He stands up and jumps so high in the air that he could've dunked on a basketball backboard.

"Ian was so psyched, and he just shouted, '*Yeah*! *Yeah*!'"

And that's what it feels like to win it all. You savor it loudly, quietly, and in a smoky bar.

CHAPTER 23

Charles Woodson:
No Luck Required

Charles Woodson rushed for 2,028 yards as a senior at Fremont (Ohio) Ross. So the first time we spoke on the phone during his recruitment, I asked which side of the ball he wanted to play on in college.

"Defense," he said.

"Why?"

"Because I love to hit," he said.

Now, I talked to dozens of standout running back–defensive back combos as a reporter. I can't remember even one other such player who didn't want to play tailback at the next level. But if somehow one or two have escaped me over the years, I can assure you that there was not another 2,000-yard rusher I encountered who wanted to flatten runners instead of getting the ball in college.

In 1997, he became the only primarily defensive player to win the Heisman Trophy—beating out two of the best offensive players of their generation in Tennessee quarterback Peyton Manning and Marshall wide receiver Randy Moss.

Woodson believed playing defense would preclude him from winning a Heisman, and he definitely improved his chances by becoming a part-time offensive player in his last two seasons in Ann Arbor. Woodson was a throwback to the day of the two-way player, and the Wolverines had one of the best from that era in 1940 Heisman Trophy winner Tom Harmon.

Wolverines coach Lloyd Carr said Woodson was grounded enough

Cornerback Charles Woodson (2) intercepts a pass from Washington State's Ryan Leaf in the end zone during the first half of the 84th Rose Bowl in Pasadena, California, on Thursday, January 1, 1998. (AP Photo/ Mark J. Terrill)

coming out of high school to make a calculated decision that benefited him greatly. "In the NFL today," Carr said, "tailbacks have the shortest playing span. They take such a beating. His maturity for a 17-year-old was amazing. Charles could see that.

"People said, 'You should tell him he can be a running back.' I said, 'Clearly, he wants to be a cornerback because he wants to play in the NFL. And if he had been a running back for us, I am not certain whether or not he still would've won the Heisman Trophy."

But there is no question that Woodson juiced his Heisman chances and the Wolverines' offense by accepting Carr's invitation to moonlight on offense beginning with his sophomore season.

"Charles was hosting a recruit after his freshman year," Carr said, "and I was sitting next to him at dinner. We had just lost [receivers] Mercury Hayes and Amani Toomer in the NFL draft along with [tail-back] Tshimanga Biakabutuka, who left early. Tshimanga had a chance to win the Heisman had he stayed. So I asked Charles, 'Do you want to play some offense next fall? Do you want to play tailback?'"

Woodson replied, "No, but I will play receiver."

In his final two seasons at Michigan, Woodson had 38 offensive touches that produced 607 yards (16.0 yards per touch) and five touchdowns. He had 25 catches, 11 runs mostly on reverses, and two pass completions.

"He had explosive speed," Carr said. "Charles had a burst. So we sent him out deep at first, then worked in the intermediate stuff, and then the reverses. We developed it his sophomore year, and it wasn't much. But the idea was, 'You'd better know where he was in the game.' Each week we'd add something he had not done before, and he enjoyed it."

Woodson was like the one pupil the teacher needed to challenge with extra-credit reports to assure maximum learning and growth. "After the team movie on the night before every game when I was the head coach," Carr said, "I would go to every room in the hotel and briefly talk to every player. I would say, 'Good luck tomorrow, and good night.' It was a fun thing for me, and a chance to be completely different with a player who maybe I had been on all week.

"I liked that: 'Good luck tomorrow, and good night.' One night, I went in to say that to Charles. He smiled, looked back at me, and said, 'Coach, I don't need any luck.'"

Carr removed the Michigan baseball cap from his head, smiled, and scratched his head.

"And," Carr said, "he didn't."

Charles Woodson didn't need any luck. He was that good.

Woodson edged Tennessee quarterback Peyton Manning—who incidentally took a visit to Michigan in the class before Woodson's—for the Heisman in a close vote. Woodson had 1,815 points and 433 first-place votes to 1,543 points and 281 firsts for Manning.

He had eight interceptions and 44 tackles on defense, winning his second consecutive consensus All-America recognition as well as becoming the most decorated defensive player in the history of the game.

Woodson also won the Walter Camp, Bronko Nagurski, Chuck Bednarik, Jim Thorpe, and Jack Tatum awards. And, taking it up another notch, Woodson also took home the 1998 Big Ten Jesse Owens Athlete of the Year. He also won the Big Ten Defensive Player of the Year Award—now called the Nagurski-Woodson Big Ten Defensive Player of the Year Award.

He has been the purest all-around football player in the last half-century—the one and only player who did virtually everything since two-way football players were phased out in the 1960s.

Woodson's three biggest games in 1997 came against his school's two arch-rivals and in the Rose Bowl win over Washington State that wrapped up a 12–0 season and the Associated Press national championship. Against the Spartans, he made two interceptions, including his most dramatic defensive play of the year—an acrobatic, leaping, one-handed interception near the sideline in East Lansing. He struck fear into opponents by making plays that left you shaking your head and saying, "How did he do that?"

Against the Buckeyes, he made the three key plays in a 20–14 win: an interception in the end zone, a 37-yard reception from Brian Griese that set up the lone offensive touchdown, and a 78-yard punt return touchdown. Woodson intended to do the Heisman pose, a la Desmond Howard, but he was engulfed by teammates before he could get his arms extended.

"I kept telling him not to do it," Carr said, "but he was going to do it."

Yet it was a game that could've ended before any of the heroics by Woodson.

Ohio State receiver David Boston had made boastful claims leading up to the game. He predicted a three-touchdown victory and noted that All-American Woodson was not as good as Buckeyes cornerback

Antoine Winfield. In 1998, Winfield was an All-America selection and won the Jim Thorpe Award and Jack Tatum Trophy—both of which Woodson won as the top defensive back in 1997.

Boston, from Humble (Texas) High, had visited Michigan while Woodson and strong safety Marcus Ray were freshmen, and talked trash with them while informing them that he was going to Ohio State.

Woodson and Boston got into it early in the game when Boston ran a route toward the left sideline and Woodson played him tightly. The pass did not come Boston's way, and he stopped looking for the ball, and instead began shoving Woodson, who shoved back. Boston grabbed Woodson's facemask and yanked. Woodson took off the helmet and gave Boston an earful.

"There had been all that build-up with Boston," Carr said. "And he instigated it by pulling Charles' facemask. But the official did a great thing. For taking his helmet off, Charles could have been thrown out of the game. But I think it was good he didn't get thrown out."

Had Woodson been ejected, Michigan likely would not have won the game in which it took a 20–0 lead before winning by six points, and Woodson probably would not have won the Heisman. His signature game and defining play, the punt return touchdown, never would have played out.

Boston dropped two passes but caught a 56-yard touchdown pass despite good coverage from Woodson. But there was no saving face with that. Woodson controlled the game and afterward walked off the field with a long-stemmed red rose in his teeth.

"They do all the talkin'," Woodson said, walking off and looking into a television camera. "I do the walkin', baby."

And then there was that December 1, 1997, *Sports Illustrated* cover with Boston dropping to the ground after being upended by Ray, who shoved both of his legs out from under him on a pass break-up. The headline read, "Take That!" The subhead added, "No. 1 Michigan Flattens Ohio State."

Hitting the ground knocked the wind out of Boston, and Ray had this message for him: "Don't you ever talk trash in the Big House—ever again."

Michigan walked the walk all the way to Pasadena where Woodson confounded Washington State quarterback Ryan Leaf in a 21–16 Wolverines victory that sewed up the No. 1 ranking in the final Associated Press poll.

Woodson picked off Leaf, who would become the second overall pick in the draft by the San Diego Chargers behind Manning, and broke up four of his passes while making one tackle behind the line of scrimmage.

It was the last of 18 interceptions and 162 tackles Woodson made at Michigan. He would've had little to prove as a senior and entered the NFL draft.

The Oakland Raiders took him fourth overall in the first round, and he wasted no time in establishing himself. Woodson is a nine-time Pro Bowl pick; was named to the NFL's All–2000s team of the decade; was the NFL's Defensive Player of the Year in 2009; has 55 interceptions and 937 tackles; and he won a Super Bowl with the Green Bay Packers, who signed him for seven years and $52 million in 2006. He played with them through the 2012 season.

And so, that calculated move Carr watched Woodson make in 1995 has paid off in every way.

Playing defense surprisingly resulted in Woodson winning the Heisman, but it also figured into that long NFL career he had in mind. He has played 15 distinguished seasons as a pro. And in 2009 he donated $2 million to the C.S. Mott Children's Hospital in Ann Arbor. He established the Charles C. Woodson Scholarship for an incoming freshman kinesiology major who has financial needs and shows outstanding academic promise.

He has given back and received everything he could have hoped for in the game.

Charles Woodson might not have needed any luck, but the Wolverines were certainly lucky to have him. His legacy will be an enduring one.

THE TEAM WITH 31 FUTURE NFL PLAYERS

Perhaps the most mind-blowing fact connected to Michigan's 1997 national championship team is that 31 of them played in the NFL. And seven of them played for a decade or longer in a league where the average player lasts just over three years.

Woodson heads the list of those playing more than 10 seasons in the NFL. Joining him are quarterback Brian Griese, offensive tackle Jon Jansen, tight ends Jerame Tuman and Mark Campbell, and linebackers Dhani Jones and James Hall.

Tuman and rugged defensive end Glen Steele joined Woodson as consensus All-Americans on that '97 Dream Team. Steele also had a confident yet comforting reply for Carr when he made the rounds at the team hotel on Friday nights before games with his "good night, good luck" message.

Carr said, "Steele would tell me, 'Get some sleep, Coach. We'll take care of this one.'"

They did not get to settle matters once and for all in a championship game with Nebraska, which finished atop the *USA Today*/ESPN Coaches Poll. But they did meet the Cornhuskers.

Michigan, which was No. 1 in the final Associated Press poll, and Nebraska both visited the White House after splitting the 1997 national championships. That was the final season before the BCS bowl system was implemented.

"Everybody wanted Michigan and Nebraska to meet," President Clinton said while hosting the two teams. "I'm the only one who could pull it off."

CHAPTER 24

Why Quarterback Scot Loeffler Became More Than a Friend for Life to Brian Griese and Tom Brady

Quarterback Scot Loeffler never threw a pass or took a snap in a game at Michigan, and yet he had a significant impact on the teams he was part of from 1993–96 and beyond.

Loeffler was voted the No. 9 prospect on the *Detroit Free Press* Best of the Midwest team selected by major college recruiting coordinators, and Wolverines head coach Lloyd Carr said Loeffler might have had more talent than any of the accomplished quarterbacks who were his teammates. But a shoulder injury ended his career prematurely, and he took to helping the team from behind the scenes.

Brian Griese and Tom Brady, who remain close friends years later, benefited from Loeffler's support and instruction as a teammate and coach. He also later served as the Wolverines' quarterbacks coach, tutoring Chad Henne, John Navarre, Drew Henson, and Brady.

And when Urban Meyer hired Loeffler as his quarterbacks coach at Florida, Tim Tebow led the NCAA in passing efficiency in that 2009 season.

"Scot had a great impact on all of those quarterbacks," said former Michigan offensive coordinator Mike DeBord who oversaw Loeffler as both a player and coach. "First, it was as a student assistant. Then he was a graduate assistant before becoming the quarterbacks coach. Not only was he close to Tom and Brian, but he started working with them when they were peers.

"Scot was so smart and knows the position so well. But it was important that he had the relationships with these guys first.

"When Scot got hurt, Brian became the guy in that class. And Scot played through Brian in the years ahead. He looked at it like Brian Griese was playing for him. He was close with Brian and Tom Brady. And they are still close today. Scot was like brothers to those guys, and all the work Scot put into helping them helped make them the players they became."

Griese came to Michigan as a walk-on from Christopher Columbus High in Miami, and Loeffler was an All-American at Barberton (Ohio) High, alma mater of legendary Michigan coach Bo Schembechler. Loeffler was a big quarterback—6'4" and 200 pounds—with a big arm, and he was considered the premier quarterback in a football-rich state.

Many elite athletes would have found it too painful to remain that close to something they could not touch themselves, but Loeffler defined what a true teammate is by giving everything he had to offer and putting aside the need for personal glory.

DeBord instituted some subtle changes in the offense when Griese left after winning the 1997 national championship in order to tailor the offense to Brady.

"Most fans didn't notice a thing changing when the offense went from Griese to Brady, but there were changes," DeBord said. "Brian was very accurate and got rid of the ball quickly. He could do things on the perimeter, and we tried to control the ball more with Brian. Because of Brady's lack of ability to get out of the pocket, we threw the ball downfield more with Tom. And Tom had a great pocket presence, too.

"It was really a tremendous honor to coach all of those guys. Michigan is so special, and sometimes people do not realize it until they are gone."

DeBord took Loeffler with him as the quarterbacks coach when he became the Central Michigan head coach in 2000, but Loeffler returned to Ann Arbor two years later to join Carr's staff as a full-time assistant and quarterbacks coach. After Carr retired, Loeffler spent a year coaching quarterbacks for the Detroit Lions in 2008 and then spent two years with the Gators.

Loeffler was the offensive coordinator at Temple in 2011, Auburn in 2012, and joined Virginia Tech coach Frank Beamer as his offensive coordinator for the 2013 season.

In the 1993 Michigan football media guide, Loeffler listed his intent to attend law school and become an attorney. But by giving of himself and feeling the satisfaction of making others better, Loeffler found his true calling. And in doing so, Loeffler became the wind beneath the wings of some pretty high-flying quarterbacks.

CHAPTER 25

Tom Brady:
From Fifth String to Superstar

Tom Brady began his career at Michigan as the fifth-string quarterback. Blows your mind, doesn't it?

There are those who thought he might have been better off signing with baseball's Montreal Expos, who drafted the power-hitting catcher from San Mateo (California) Junipero Serra in the 18th round in 1995. Baseball scouts believed he would have been drafted much higher had it not been for his football scholarship, and they loved his arm and intangibles.

Serra, an all-boys Catholic school located south of San Francisco, is a sports powerhouse. It has produced Barry Bonds, Jim Fregosi, and Gregg Jefferies in baseball, and Lynn Swann in football.

So there was a legacy for Brady to follow in both sports—especially in baseball. However, the Expos never got into serious negotiations with Brady because he and his parents, Galynn and Tom Sr., had decided they wanted him to go to college.

Brady, though, was not an All-American quarterback in high school. He was a good-looking prospect with a strong arm, touch, and a good head, and he was recruited to fill the bill as the quarterback the Wolverines seek in every class.

The man who would take the New England Patriots to five Super Bowls and tie the record for quarterback starts with John Elway did not become the established starter at Michigan until he was a red-shirt junior. After two seasons, the quarterback who would throw for 44,806 yards and 334 touchdowns in his first 13 NFL seasons threw for 129 yards with zero touchdowns. But he broke out during his fourth year on campus.

Most quarterbacks who set the NFL on fire leave college after three or four years. But Brady stayed five years and was only a sixth-round pick by the Patriots in 2000. However, when Drew Bledsoe went down during Brady's rookie season, Brady stepped up big-time—and the rest is history.

There were plenty of players in front of him when he was a freshman in 1995: Scott Dreisbach, Brian Griese, Jason Carr, and Scot Loeffler. Two of those quarterbacks would play in the NFL, but none had the sort of universal acclaim coming out of high school to scare off Brady. Though, Peyton Manning might very well have sent Brady in another direction with another school. Manning made an official visit to Ann Arbor and would have been behind senior Todd Collins as a freshman in 1994 had he selected the Wolverines. But Manning chose Tennessee, where he began his freshman season as a third-stringer behind future Colorado Rockies slugger Todd Helton and Jerry Colquitt. Both got injured, and Manning earned a chance to start that he never relinquished.

Manning threw for 11,201 yards and 89 touchdowns—both Tennessee records. But he finished second in the 1997 Heisman Trophy voting to Charles Woodson, who could've been his teammate at Michigan.

Imagine that.

There was also a great player coming in behind Brady—one that received attention that rivaled Manning's coming out of high school. Drew Henson was considered perhaps the finest quarterback the state of Michigan had ever produced, and the Brighton High three-sport star committed to Coach Lloyd Carr after his junior season of 1996.

I was covering the Detroit Tigers in 1999 when Henson and Brady would compete once again for the starting position that nearly everyone conceded to Henson.

Perhaps the only person in the state who thought otherwise was

Tigers infielder Jefferies, a two-time All-Star in his prime with the St. Louis Cardinals who also went to Serra and had been around Brady for years.

"Brady is better than Henson, you watch," Jefferies said.

I told him that loyalty is a wonderful thing and that I could understand him supporting one of his own. But Henson—who also played minor league baseball for the New York Yankees while at Michigan after they drafted him in the third round—was just something special. Surely he could not be beat out by anyone—let alone Brady.

But what did I know?

Oddly enough, although Henson was heralded and Brady developed,

New England Patriots quarterback Tom Brady greets Lloyd Carr, his coach during his playing days at the University of Michigan, before playing the Cleveland Browns in an NFL football game on Sunday, November 7, 2010, in Cleveland. (AP Photo/Amy Sancetta)

both were sixth round picks in the NFL draft—Henson was selected by the Houston Texans in 2003. And both would back up Bledsoe. Henson fell in behind Bledsoe and a young Tony Romo with the Dallas Cowboys in 2005, one year after giving up on baseball after achieving just one career major league hit.

When Brady met Patriots owner Bob Kraft for the first time, he thanked him and sincerely noted that taking him would be one of the best things Mr. Kraft's club had ever done. A statement like that would be going out on the limb for 99.9 percent of first-round picks. But a sixth-round pick? C'mon.

Brady developed confidence, mental toughness, and dedication to staying the course at Michigan that would benefit him for years to come. He hired a sports psychologist to cope with the frustrations and anxieties caused by his failure to make an early impact with the Wolverines, and he considered transferring closer to home to Cal-Berkeley.

"No doubt, Tom was close to packing it in and leaving," said Mike DeBord, who was Michigan's offensive coordinator when Brady flourished. "It was hard for Tom to share playing time, but he always handled that with class. I don't know why he stayed, but every Michigan fan is glad he did."

Brady did not want to fail and stuck it out, and he said numerous times that those trials helped prepare him for the challenges he would meet in the NFL and in his life. And eventually, the quarterback buried on the depth chart began burying opponents. Brady mostly carried a clipboard during the 1997 national championship season when he played behind Griese. But once he got the reins, Brady went 20–5 as a starter and led the team to a co-Big Ten championship in 1998.

Brady was all about winning. He helped the Patriots set the NFL record with 21 consecutive wins in 2003–04, holds the league record with 17 playoff wins, and has won three Super Bowls and two Super Bowl MVP Awards.

Brady was named *Sports Illustrated*'s Sportsman of the Year in 2005 and was selected for eight Pro Bowl teams. But an honorable mention All-Big Ten selection in 1999 was the best he could muster in college despite putting up some pretty good numbers in his final two seasons during which he passed for 5,222 yards and 35 touchdowns.

If you are looking for a good sports trivia stumper, ask for the name of the Big Ten's first-team quarterback selected ahead of both Brady and Drew Brees in 1999. The All-Big Ten first-team quarterback on teams voted upon by both the coaches and the media that year was Ohio State's Joe Germaine. The second-team choice was Purdue's Brees, who also became an NFL superstar with the New Orleans Saints, and Brady was an honorable mention pick by the coaches.

Brady was a team captain as a senior when he threw for a school bowl record 369 yards and four touchdowns in a 35–34 overtime win over Alabama in the Orange Bowl on January 1, 2000. He beat Ohio State, Penn State, and Notre Dame that season, but losses to Michigan State and unranked Illinois were the blemishes of a 10–2 record. The Wolverines finished ranked fifth in a season that could have been better, but there was much more in store for Brady at the next level.

He threw an NFL-record 50 touchdown passes with only eight interceptions for 4,806 yards in 2007 when he won the first of two NFL MVP awards. Brady repeated the honor in 2010.

And he became a rock star–like celebrity, as well.

Brady has appeared on the cover of *GQ*, hosted *Saturday Night Live,* and married supermodel Gisele Bundchen. He has transcended sports by becoming a pop culture figure, and the only football players to surpass him that way have been Joe Namath and O.J. Simpson.

Not bad for a fifth-string quarterback who rose to honorable mention all-conference status before becoming a sixth-round draft pick.

Brady surpassed expectations at every turn on his way to stardom, and now he has taken his game to such a level that nothing short of a Super Bowl win is expected. He's had a storybook career even before the final chapters are written.

CHAPTER 26

Hart, Henne, Long, and Eight Miles of Total Offense

Living large was what Chad Henne, Mike Hart, and Jake Long did at Michigan.

The Wolverines have never had a quarterback as productive as Henne, a tailback who gained more yards than Hart, or an offensive tackle who drove defenders into submission like Long. And they all played together for four seasons beginning in 2004 when they were the young guard on one of the scariest offensive machines to ever come through the Big Ten.

Braylon Edwards, the most prolific pass-catcher in school history and winner of the Biletnikoff Award as college football's top receiver, and David Baas, the school's lone Rimington Trophy winner as the nation's top center, were the heart of the old guard that season.

They led the Wolverines to that comeback, a 45–37 triple-overtime win over Michigan State en route to a Big Ten co-championship and a wild ride that ended with a 38–37 Rose Bowl loss to Texas and quarterback Vince Young.

Hart and Henne combined to rush and pass for nearly 15,000 yards—that's about 8-1/2 miles of offense. And Long threw the key blocks almost every mile of the way.

Long would join Heisman Trophy winner Tom Harmon as the school's only No. 1 overall picks in the NFL draft, but a tragedy nearly kept him from ever reaching the field at the Big House. He could have lost his career or his life in a house fire after completing his freshman

Offensive lineman Jake Long (77) (left), quarterback Chad Henne (center), and running back Mike Hart (20) (right), pose for a portrait at Michigan's Media Day on Monday, August 6, 2007, in Ann Arbor, Michigan. (AP Photo/Tony Ding)

year as a red-shirted player. Long had to bust out of the second story, jump onto a car below, and then survive a long hospital stay as black, smoke-infested phlegm was suctioned out of his lungs through tubes.

Hart issued his infamous "little brother" comment to light a fire under Michigan State, guaranteed victory over Notre Dame, and made Coach Lloyd Carr's all-time "trash talk" trio for the Wolverines. He was the little big man on campus, and retired Michigan sports information department football liaison Jim Schneider said the feisty runner listed at 5'9" and 188 lbs. "might have been" 5'8" with "real long spikes" on his cleats.

Henne, born in Wyomissing, Pennsylvania, came to the Wolverines despite being the prime target of Penn State coach Joe Paterno and also visiting Miami, Tennessee, and Georgia. He started as a true freshman after No. 1 quarterback Matt Gutierrez's shoulder failed him one week before the 2004 opener and moved ahead of future San Diego Padres pitcher Clayton Richard on the depth chart by making a quick impression on Carr. He would not only put up big yards but lead some amazing comebacks. "Never say die" was his mantra.

They all went out with the retiring Carr on January 1, 2008, winning the Capital One Bowl in Orlando against Heisman Trophy winner Tim Tebow and Florida coach Urban Meyer. They helped carry Carr off the field on their shoulders after a 41–35 triumph, and their relationships remain close to this day.

"Florida had a great team with Tim Tebow and Percy Harvin," Carr said. "They won the national championship the year before, and they would win the national championship the season after they played us. That was a team that was loaded, and we were huge underdogs [10½ points].

"To win that last game with that group of seniors was really special. They kept teams together through incredibly tough times and beat a special team in their last game. And we played absolutely as well as we could in that game. That meant a lot to me. There were a couple turnovers, but we played as well as I could've hoped."

I asked Carr for his thoughts while riding out on their shoulders. "I was happy because all of those kids were happy," he said. "We beat Tebow in Florida."

And that terrific trio has stayed close to Carr while playing in the NFL and, in the case of Hart, beginning his own coaching career as the running backs coach just down the road in Ypsilanti at Eastern Michigan under head coach and former Wolverines defensive coordinator Ron English.

Carr lit up when talking about them. He recalled going to a game in Miami with his wife, Laurie, when Brady and his New England Patriots were in town to play the Dolphins, who drafted Henne in the second round after making Long the top overall pick in the 2008 NFL Draft.

"On every play in that game," Carr said, "a Michigan quarterback took the snap. Chad played great in that game. And after the game, Chad and his wife and Jake and his wife went out with us to a steakhouse. We had a great time; it was special. Chad's wife is a very dear woman, and she was telling some stories about Chad."

Chad and Brittany had dated since they were 14 and attended West Lawn (Pennsylvania) Wilson High.

"And then there was the time Jake had been out all night," Carr said. "He left a message on my phone at 6:00 AM, and he was singing. Jake was singing that song, 'Sunrise, Sunset!'"

Carr leaned back on a bench and took a break from eating a deli sandwich. He shook his head, and his eyes twinkled.

"Jake finished up the message," Carr said. "He said, 'Coach, we wish you were here. I love you.'"

"Sunrise, Sunset," from *Fiddler on the Roof*, ends this way:

Sunrise, sunset,
swiftly fly the years,
one season following another,
laden with happiness,
and tears.

Maybe Jake Long singing like Tevye in the wedding scene is a stretch, but it worked for Carr. He was touched by the sentiment of a man he was always there for—at the lowest and highest points of his college life.

On June 16, 2004, Long was living with several football players in a two-story house rented just east of State Street and not far from Schembechler Hall. That night, the Detroit Pistons beat the Los Angeles Lakers to clinch the NBA Championship in Auburn Hills, northeast of Ann Arbor. Celebrations broke out throughout the area, and investigators surmised that fireworks exploding in the area started a fire that burned down the house Long lived in with offensive guard and close friend Adam Kraus, placekicker Garrett Rivas, and others.

"Jake knocked out a window and jumped off the second floor after battling through all the smoke and flames," Carr said. "He landed on a teammate's car.

"[Running backs coach] Fred Jackson called me at 2:30 AM and said there was a fire in a house some of the players stayed in. I asked if everybody got out, and he said, 'Yeah.' I got there about 3:00 AM, and the first thing I see is Jake on his back on a gurney. He was telling the nurse, 'I'm fine. I just want to go home.' Flames were still raging in the house fire. Jake was adamant, saying, 'I do not want to go to the hospital.'

"The nurse said, 'You've got to tell him that he needs to go.' That girl saved his life."

And she did so with an assist from his head coach.

"If he was not Jake Long," Schneider said, "he'd have died. He had to knock out a locked door to get out the window. Police were surprised no one died."

Carr said, "Then in the hospital, he had all these tubes suctioning all of this black stuff out of his lungs. He was in the hospital for two weeks."

Long played in the opener and started eight games that fall for a Big Ten co-champion. His career was off and running. Long, from Lapeer (Michigan) East High, was a 6'7", 316-lb. giant with the speed and reflexes of a baseball first baseman and basketball post man—which he was in high school.

"You don't find many offensive tackles that played baseball," Carr said. Although Greg Skrepenak was another Wolverines All-American offensive tackle who played first base. "Not only was he big with all kinds of athletic ability, but he was very smart and as tough as this floor."

Carr tapped his shoe heel on the concrete flooring.

"Jake missed [seven] games his junior year," Carr said of 2005, when Long was using his second year of eligibility. "[Trainer] Paul Schmidt said, 'Lloyd, he won't be back; don't expect him back.' His mom and dad came up that night, and I visited with them at the Sheraton. A high ankle sprain can be worse than a break. Jake looked at me and said, 'Coach, I will be back.' And he came back. Against Iowa, we would've had a hard time winning that game without Jake Long."

Long was the lead blocker on Jerome Jackson's overtime touchdown run that beat the Hawkeyes in Iowa City. He injured his foot two games later against Indiana but wore a protective boot off the field and played against Ohio State. He took on Buckeyes linebacker Bobby Carpenter, who would be taken in the first round by the Dallas Cowboys that April, on a play that resulted in a broken foot for Carpenter. However, Long was also hobbled by hits taken in that game, and it was feared he would require surgery and miss the Alamo Bowl. But he played through the injury against Nebraska in that game in San Antonio.

However, as frustrating as that 7–5 season was for Long and all of the Wolverines, everything came together in 2006. Long cut weight from 338 to 316 lbs. to gain increased agility, speed, and endurance. He moved from the right tackle position to the most valuable spot on the line—left tackle, the blind-side protector of the right-handed-throwing Henne. Long thrived, was selected as an All-American, and Michigan was 11–0 and ranked No. 2 before taking on No. 1 Ohio State in a true classic. The Wolverines lost 42–39 and also squandered a clear shot at the national championship.

Some believed a rematch game between the Buckeyes and Michigan in the BCS championship game was warranted, but Florida got the nod and upset Ohio State in that game in Glendale, Arizona. And the Wolverines were thumped 32–18 by Southern Cal in the Rose Bowl. The Gators won the title that few imagined possible.

Long decided to pass on a sure first-round selection in the upcoming NFL draft and had another All-American season. He was also a finalist for the Outland Trophy as the nation's outstanding interior lineman.

"Jake Long became a dominating player," Carr said. "He was devoid of any weakness. When he locked on you with a block, he would take

Quarterback Chad Henne throws against Notre Dame in South Bend, Indiana, on Saturday, September 16, 2006. Henne threw for three touchdowns and 220 yards as Michigan defeated Notre Dame 47-21. (AP Photo/Michael Conroy)

guys 10 and 15 yards down the field. Jake was a first-round pick after 2006, and I expected he would leave after that year. But he came into my office one day and said, 'Coach, I'm staying.' Wow. That was a hell of a thing for our recruiting. It was so much like [offensive tackle] Taylor Lewan deciding to stay [for his senior season in 2013]."

Pro Football Hall of Fame coach Bill Parcells was four months into his final NFL position as vice president of football operations for the Miami Dolphins when he called Carr about Long and the upcoming draft.

"Parcells called me and wanted to talk a lot about Jake and Henne," Carr said. "On Jake, Parcells said, 'Is this guy as good as I think he is?' I said, 'Coach, he's unbelievable—a great player and a great leader.' Parcells wanted to know more about him. We talked some more and then he said, 'Pass along this message: He can be the first player taken in the NFL draft. It's a real special thing, and I want him to be a Dolphin.'"

But there was a matter of being able to sign him for what the Dolphins had in mind. And there was also the challenge of getting Long pumped up about playing for a team that had been 1–15 the previous season under former Wolverines offensive assistant coach Cam Cameron in his lone season as head coach.

"Part of it was going around Jake's agent," Carr said. Long was represented by experienced agent Tom Condon. "But it worked out great for Jake with a Hall of Famer deciding to make him the first pick. If he'd gone after his junior year, Jake would not have made near the money he got."

He became the third offensive tackle taken No. 1 overall, joining Pro Football Hall of Famer Ron Yary of Southern Cal in 1968 and Ohio State's Orlando Pace in 1997. And Long made good on the five-year contract he signed out of college for $57.75 million. He was selected for the Pro Bowl in all five seasons with the Dolphins before leaving as a free agent to sign with the St. Louis Rams, getting a four-year contract for $36 million in 2013.

However, Long's decision to play his senior year resulted in more than just tens of millions of dollars for him. It also influenced Hart in staying for his final season—during which he would rush for 100 yards or more another nine times to push his school-record total in that category to 28 games.

Hart carried the ball more often (1,015 carries) for more yards (5,040) than anybody who ever wore the Maize and Blue of Michigan. He finished fifth in 2006 Heisman Trophy voting and was a little pack of dynamite that exploded defenses week after week, year after year.

"Hart had as much great self-confidence as anybody," Carr said. "He was fearless and such a fierce competitor. And he was smart as a whip with great instincts, great feet, and great vision. He was also an excellent receiver and an excellent pass protector. And because he was so quick and had all of those abilities, he was able to avoid big hits."

Carr said Hart rivaled 2001 All-American linebacker Larry Foote and Marcus Ray, a safety on the 1997 national championship team, in another interesting category.

"Larry Foote, Marcus Ray, and Mike Hart were the biggest trash-talkers we ever had," Carr said, forcing a smile and shaking his head. "It was something that was very much discouraged, but it's part of a guy's personality. On the field, it's nothing really. A lot of it goes on. But it adds to the intensity of a game and motivates.

"Mike, he wanted to win so badly. He was an outstanding team guy and fun to watch. But that was just part of who he was."

Hart saved his most memorable mouthing for 2007. After the 0–2 start, he guaranteed victory over Notre Dame and the result was a 38–0 shellacking of the Fighting Irish. And then, after making a key play in a 28–24 comeback win that made it six straight over intrastate rival Michigan State, he uttered the boastful words that are linked to him perhaps more than his rushing records.

Hart said, "Sometimes it's just like when you're playing your little brother in basketball. You let him get a lead and let him get excited, but then you take it back from him."

Spartans coach Mark Dantonio was peeved about the comment.

"I won't comment on that, you know," he said at the time before continuing. "I guess I can't help myself. It's not over. I'm going to be a coach here for a long time. It's just starting."

Michigan State won four straight over Michigan after that game.

"There has always been a lot of talk between Michigan and Michigan State," Carr said. "It's part of the rivalry. And Mark Dantonio's made a big issue out of it. What impact it had, I don't know for sure. But I don't think it helped us."

Carr took a deep breath and he frowned. The Wolverines didn't beat the Spartans again until 2012, and he believes that Hart's comment definitely impacted the series turnaround. The coach added that there were plenty of undercurrents behind Hart making the "little brother" comment back in 2007.

"It was such a great win up there [in East Lansing]," Carr said, "And the team took a lot of abuse after the start of that season."

Losing the opener to Appalachian State was so devastating that it dropped the Wolverines completely out of the Associated Press poll after beginning the season No. 5. Then they lost by 32 points to Oregon. The team was in a complete state of humiliation. But it had somehow risen from the dead, winning seven in a row going into that Michigan State game.

Carr played Hart sparingly in the second half after taking a 14–3 lead, but the Spartans rallied with Hart out to take a 24–14 lead with just less than eight minutes remaining. Michigan's chances were hanging by a thread, and then Henne got hurt. Much-heralded freshman quarterback Ryan Mallett came in and fumbled the first snap.

That could have been it for the Wolverines.

"But Hart picks up the fumble and runs for a first down!" Carr said. "It's a play I'll never forget."

That dramatic play sparked Michigan, and Henne came back to

throw touchdown passes to Greg Mathews and future New York Giants Super Bowl hero Mario Manningham to pull out an unlikely victory.

Hart rushed for 110 yards on 15 carries and finished four games against the Spartans with 672 yards rushing and four wins. Yet without his fumble recovery and Henne returning to pull it out of the fire, "little brother" never would have been born.

And here's an interesting note on that fumble from Carr: "Now, I've never seen anyone with a bigger arm than Ryan Mallett. But Ryan played in an offense [at Texas High in Texarkana, Texas] that was entirely out of the shotgun. We had to teach him how to take a snap, and he struggled with that all year."

Mallett, rated the No. 2 drop-back passer in his high school class by Rivals.com, would pass for 892 yards and seven touchdowns as the backup through Henne's injury-riddled senior season. But Henne wasn't going to leave this rivalry game to Mallett no matter how much he ached.

"Chad hurt his shoulder at Michigan State," Carr said, "but he comes back and wins that game for us. He was not healthy until the Florida game when he played the best game he ever played."

Henne completed 25-of-39 passes for 373 yards and three touchdowns against the Gators, throwing the go-ahead TD pass with 4:12 remaining and beating out Tebow for Capital One Bowl MVP honors.

The Wolverines at the time had a long line of successful NFL quarterbacks from Jim Harbaugh to Tom Brady with Elvis Grbac, Todd Collins, and Brian Griese in between. But the numbers Henne put up dwarfed them all. Henne completed 828-of-1,387 passes for 9,715 yards and 87 touchdowns—all records. Henne completed seven fewer passes than Grbac attempted and completed more passes than Brady or Harbaugh attempted.

"He had a great arm and was big and strong," Carr said. "We ran a complicated system in terms of what a quarterback was expected to do. Our quarterback had to tell every guy in the huddle what to do with code words like 'Red' and 'Zane.' He had to give them the formation and the protection and possibly check out of the play. If he checked out, he had to go through all of that again—and in 25 seconds."

The fact that he was such a quick study and was able to start when Gutierrez went down ended up being critical to the success of the 2004 team. Henne joined Rick Leach (1975) as the only true freshmen to start at quarterback for the Wolverines.

"We were going to redshirt him as a freshman until Gutierrez got hurt," Carr said. "But Henne took his first team to the Rose Bowl as a freshman. And in his last bowl game as a senior, he was just incredible. Chad was as even-keeled as any player I had, and [he] took great pride in preparation."

Henne spent four seasons with the Dolphins before signing a two-year contract with the Jacksonville Jaguars in 2012. But he's thrown more interceptions (48) than touchdowns (42) and passed for a modest 9,198 yards in the NFL. Henne also has yet to start for a team with a winning record.

Carr pursed his lips and grasped the handle of his coffee cup, pausing for an instant. Then he looked up and said, "You know, I hope Chad gets a chance to play for a good team. I think then he will show people what he can do."

Carr remains in Henne's corner, just as he has for countless other players he's coached. In many ways, players are to coaches what children are to parents. The time to leave home or leave your team eventually comes, but a bond develops that forever keeps them in one another's thoughts and hopes.

Love develops from the relationships. And one morning, if he's really fortunate, a coach wakes up and listens to a former player singing on a phone voicemail message, affirming just how special their time together was.

CHAPTER 27

Three Bitter Defeats:

The Texas Rose Bowl Shoot-Out, Losing to No. 1 in Columbus, and Colorado's Miracle

Lloyd Carr experienced three bitter defeats at Michigan.

There was the most dramatic one—the 64-yard Hail Mary touchdown pass by Colorado quarterback Kordell Stewart at the Big House in 1994. There was the most significant one—the high-scoring loss to No. 1 Ohio State with the No. 2 team in the country at Columbus in 2006. And there was the toughest one to take—the roller-coaster defeat at the hands of Texas and quarterback Vince Young in the 2005 Rose Bowl.

"To lose to Texas on the last play," Carr said, "I never had a tougher loss."

Carr paused and leaned back, letting the significance of his own words sink in. He measured it for an instant before finally reaching confirmation.

"I never had a tougher loss," Carr concluded.

He looked me in the eye, and I could see the pain of that defeat revisiting him.

"Our guys played their asses off in that game," Carr said.

Michigan receiver and kick returner Steve Breaston broke the Rose Bowl all-purpose yardage record set in 1969 by Southern Cal Heisman Trophy winner O.J. Simpson with six kickoff returns for 221 yards and 315 total yards.

Wolverines quarterback Chad Henne threw for four touchdowns, and Young countered by running for four touchdowns and passing for another for the Longhorns.

The score was tied three times, and the lead changed hands six times. Young's 23-yard touchdown run made it 35–34 for Texas. But Garrett Rivas' third field goal, a 42-yarder with 3:04 to play, made it 37–35 for Michigan. It also tied the Rose Bowl record for field goals in one game.

But could the Wolverines deny Young on the following possession, with the outcome on the line? They finally kept Young out of the end zone, but walk-on kicker Dusty Mangum's wobbly 37-yard field-goal attempt on the game's final play was true. And it was a dagger in the heart to Carr and his players.

The Rose Bowl scoreboard flashed: Texas 38, Michigan 37.

"Thirty-seven points should have been enough to win," Carr said. "There are no excuses."

However, the year before, 39 points were not enough to beat the

Mike Hart (20) outruns the Ohio State defense for a touchdown on Saturday, November 18, 2006, during the third quarter in Columbus, Ohio. (AP Photo/Jay LaPrete)

top-ranked Buckeyes.

On November 18, 2006, on the day after Bo Schembechler died before taping a segment for the *Big Ten Ticket* pregame show at WXYZ-TV in Southfield, Michigan, the team he lived for lost to his most bitter rival 42–39.

"We tried to fight for him," said Henne, who came to know Bo along with the other players. The legendary coach frequently spoke with them as individuals, and he gave regular speeches to them as a group.

Bo had addressed the team the night before he died of the terminal stages of severe heart disease. And his speech was not about the game but rather focused on imploring them to be the kind of Michigan Man that Tom Slade, the quarterback of his 1972 Rose Bowl team, had been. Slade had died of leukemia four days before Bo addressed the Wolverines prior to their biggest game.

There were never two more emotional days for Michigan than those two, and losing Bo and the first game of this century to be dubbed "The Game of the Century" was draining. The frenzied excitement of the week gave way to emptiness followed by more emptiness.

Henne threw for 267 yards and two touchdowns, and his two-point conversion pass to Breaston cut it to 42–39 with 2:16 remaining. However, Buckeyes receiving star Ted Ginn Jr. recovered the onside kick, and all that remained for the Wolverines was the final gun and a defeat that would end their national championship hopes.

The game's pivotal play came after Mike Hart opened the fourth quarter with a one-yard touchdown run—his third score in a game in which he rushed for a game-high 142 yards—that cut Ohio State's lead to 35–31. The Wolverines would have forced a punt on the Buckeyes' next possession, but linebacker and captain Shawn Crable was penalized 15 yards for a helmet-to-helmet hit on quarterback Troy Smith.

Smith, who threw for 316 yards and four touchdowns and would win the Heisman Trophy, couldn't find an open receiver as he scrambled to his right. And one step before going out of bounds to bring about fourth down, Crable dropped his head and hit the side of Smith's helmet straight on.

Given a second life on the drive, Smith took full advantage, and his 13-yard touchdown pass to Brian Robiskie provided an 11-point lead with 5:38 remaining.

With that, the Buckeyes ended up having enough points to win a game that seemed more like an Arena Football League score-fest than a game in college football's most storied rivalry—one long predicated on defense. Consider that in their games from 1971 to 1974 Ohio State and Michigan combined to score 84 points. They combined to score 81 points in this one game.

Still, it was such an appealing and evenly matched contest that many speculated the two schools could meet again in the BCS National Championship Game.

"If this was boxing," Ohio State free safety Brandon Mitchell said, "they'd definitely get a rematch."

But in another sign of how times had changed, Michigan went to the Rose Bowl for finishing second and lost to Southern Cal. Florida received the BCS bid opposite the Buckeyes and upset the Big Ten champions in Glendale, Arizona. The Wolverines ended up No. 8 in the final Associated Press poll. Most Top 10 finishes are not painful, but this one definitely hurt.

From my perspective, there was no more bitter defeat than the one that came in the Big House on September 24, 1994. I've never seen the Wolverines more crushed in defeat than after that improbable, illogical 27–26 loss to Colorado.

Many reporters had left the press box before the game's final play, and I very nearly was one of them. I picked up my notebook, stood up, and walked away from my seat. But rather than get on the elevator and head to the press conferences, I stopped and watched the last play from the top row of seats.

I took note that Michigan was rushing only three linemen—which greatly increased the chances that Stewart would be able to get off a pass. Check all the desperation touchdown passes that were successful, and very likely you will find a three-man rush. That was the case on Doug Flutie's 48-yard Hail Mary pass in 1984. The feeling most defensive coordinators share is that you drop eight into coverage and increase your chances of covering everybody and knocking down the ball. But what it often does is breathe life into an offense gasping for air.

And that was the case this time.

I mentioned that three-man rush to Carr, then the defensive coordinator, nearly 20 years later. He pursed his lips and shook his head. There was nothing more he could say about it, and the loss remained frustrating all those years later.

The six Buffaloes on the line each double-teamed one pass-rusher, and nobody got close to Stewart. He danced around, allowing his four receivers to streak to the goal line before letting fly a pass from his own 27-yard line that would come down about one yard short of the goal line. It was a 72-yard dart that found its bull's eye.

Getting it to the end zone was Stewart's job, and he accomplished it. Michael Westbrook caught the deflected ball by diving for it in the end zone with cornerback Ty Law tackling him an instant later.

"An absolutely shocking finish," ABC-TV's Keith Jackson told listeners. "...They call it the Hail Mary in some circles, and it was certainly prayerful.

"All those who were involved will never forget it—either for the joy of it or the pain of it."

Every Colorado player sprinted to the end-zone celebration and bounded like so many kids on pogo sticks. Every Michigan player looked around as if he had just lost his keys and could not find them. Linebacker Steve Morrison placed his hands on the sides of his helmet in disbelief, and receiver Amani Toomer was one of many who fell to the ground as if he had been shot and either sobbed or stayed motionless for a minute or more.

The scoreboard time clock registered all zeroes, but the scoreboard lights at the Big House were slow to recognize the miracle that had just occurred.

It read: Michigan 26, Colorado 21.

I watched the ball pop up out of the group of players who converged on it and could not tell what happened from the press box. But the Colorado players quickly made it very clear that one of them had seized the ball and the moment. Their unbridled joy made the New Year's revelers in Times Square seem sedate by comparison. And who could blame them?

Once I made my way down to the field, some of the Buffaloes had migrated to the middle of the field to take a knee and pray. It was something the team always did. Colorado coach Bill McCartney, the former Wolverines defensive coordinator, was the most visible born-again Christian coach in college football, and many of his players were or became followers of God. And I always thought that there had to be a few more converts made that day.

Several Michigan players were still prone on the ground or sitting on the grass field in disbelief while the prayer circle engaged in offering thanks.

Finally, several minutes later, the scoreboard operator decided it had to be done: Colorado 27, Michigan 26.

The Wolverines eventually wandered off to the locker room, speechless and with blank stares. After showering, dressing, and walking from the stadium with friends and family members, the conversations I had with several of them made it clear they remained in shock.

"We had a chance at a great start and already saw this one as a W," said offensive line coach Les Miles who went on to great success as the head coach at LSU. "We would've carried a lot of momentum into the Big Ten season."

They lost three conference games in what would become a disappointing season.

Free safety Chuck Winters had the best chance to alter the outcome with the ball coming down near the goal line. "I was down there and should've made the play," Winters said, "but it didn't happen. I had it in my hands."

Winters said he was coming down with the ball near the goal line when Colorado receiver Blake Anderson punched it out. Westbrook stretched out and grabbed his destiny with Law bringing him down for naught.

The NCAA has recorded games decided on final plays since 1971, and Michigan had been involved in seven, including the Colorado loss. But that was the first time it lost one of those outcomes on anything but a field goal. Defeat had never before come with no warning, no time left.

Toomer, who would leave Michigan one year later with more receiving yards than everyone but Anthony Carter, could have been the star of that game with a 65-yard touchdown catch from Todd Collins. He listened to Coach Gary Moeller's postgame talk with his teammates but couldn't remember a word of it. It was a blur during what seemed like a bad dream.

"I was too busy with my head down to hear," Toomer said.

The only player who did not seem stunned afterward was tight end Jay Riemersma who would go on to play nine years in the NFL before making an unsuccessful run in the Republican primary in 2009 for a seat in the U.S. House of Representatives in Michigan's 2nd Congressional District.

"We're all thinking of a play we want back," Riemersma said. "This is a hard one to choke down."

Moeller was frustrated at his postgame news conference but kept his voice down until leaving the Crisler Arena lounge. While waiting to do his postgame radio show in the adjoining hallway, he blurted out, "We can't sit back there and do that sloppy crap!"

There was an offside call that doomed Michigan's last drive of the game, and there was fullback Che' Foster's fourth-quarter fumble. But the sloppiness of the closing minutes culminated with nobody being able to complete the most important element in defending against the Hail Mary pass. Nobody could knock the desperation pass to the ground.

So Colorado bounded off the field in joy, and the Wolverines were left to wonder how they could have let that one slip from their grasp. There was plenty of regret after this one but no way to change it.

Winters sought out Westbrook before the Colorado bus pulled away. They clasped hands and hugged before nodding quickly and going their separate ways. They had been Little League teammates in Detroit for a 13-year-old team called the Yankees, and now they had been reunited on the agony and ecstasy of a play that will be recalled until they are old and gray.

It was a game that got away for the Wolverines, but it will never go away.

CHAPTER 28

Denard Robinson:
Bringing Joy Back to the Big House

What if Denard Robinson had decided to leave Michigan with the coach who recruited him, Rich Rodriguez?

That's certainly a sobering thought.

There definitely wouldn't have been as many smiles around Schembechler Hall and Michigan Stadium without him. And that's not just a reference to the absence of Robinson's infectious grin. All those connected to the Wolverines—fans, players, and coaches—would not have been as happy without the quarterback who brought so much joy by staying in Ann Arbor.

Brady Hoke's Sugar Bowl and Ohio State wins in his first season in 2011 quickly revived the program. But it would have been a delayed turnaround had the defense not been restored by new coordinator Greg Mattison and if Robinson had not stayed.

And nobody would have blamed Robinson for leaving. He thrived in a spread offense under Rodriguez even if the team did not. Michigan went 15–22 in Rodriguez's three seasons before he was sent packing. He had become a marquee coach at West Virginia, but he was a round peg in a square hole at Michigan, bringing in the spread offense he loved and junking the proven pro-style attack.

But whereas Rodriguez discarded the future NFL quarterback he inherited at Michigan, Ryan Mallett, Hoke embraced the great run-pass threat he was provided in Robinson. Mallett transferred to Arkansas, threw for 7,493 yards with an outstanding touchdown-to-interception ratio of 62-to-19, and finished seventh in Heisman Trophy voting in 2010.

Robinson finished sixth in Heisman balloting that same season as a sophomore when he became the first quarterback in NCAA history to exceed 2,500 yards passing and 1,500 rushing and earned the lovable nickname "Shoelace" for wearing untied football cleats and occasionally losing them on plays. But everything was changing, and some people anticipated him leaving. However, they didn't know Denard Xavier Robinson.

I asked him if he had any problem with having to make a transition between offenses and coaches.

"No," Robinson said. "I never did. I embraced it. I was going to get a chance to play in this new offense. It was an honor to work with an offensive coordinator like Al Borges, who had done all he had done. And it didn't take me long to get used to it. I like new stuff. And anytime you are working with great people, it's fun. I was improving, and it's exciting to improve."

Robinson finished his playing days ranked second in career rushing yards (4,495) and third with 42 rushing touchdowns at Michigan. He also finished fourth all-time with 6,250 yards passing and 49 touchdown passes.

But nobody in the history of Michigan football gained more than his 10,745 yards total offense or accounted for more than his 91 touchdowns via running and throwing. The only Wolverines dual-threat quarterback who compares to Robinson is Rick Leach who had 6,460 yards and 82 touchdowns (48 passing, 34 running) from 1975–78. And even Leach's yardage total was dwarfed by Robinson's.

"I talked to Rick Leach in my freshman year and watched highlights of him running and throwing the ball," Robinson said. "He was something."

Robinson not only set an NCAA single-season quarterback rushing record with 1,702 yards in 2010 but finished with the NCAA career rushing record for quarterbacks with 4,495 yards. Robinson has run with his shoelaces dangling since he was 8 years old. The Michigan equipment managers added Velcro to his shoes to keep them tight on his feet, but the nickname stuck and his elusiveness never ceased.

"[Offensive coordinator] Al Borges did a great job of getting Denard into our offense," said Hoke, who canned the spread and returned to a pro-style attack. "Denard committed to the team and to Michigan. And the enthusiasm he has for his teammates and the game of football has been so important."

When Robinson suffered ulnar nerve damage in his throwing elbow against Nebraska and could not play quarterback in his final games in 2012, he played tailback or lined up as the quarterback and handed off or ran the ball. Robinson rushed for 320 yards with a 7.0-yard average in his last three games against Iowa, Ohio State, and South Carolina.

"The amazing thing about Denard is that he was always up, even when he was hurt," Hoke said. "I'm sure that in his private moments he reflected some about what had happened to him. But you did not see that in front of his teammates."

He put his needs aside, like any good leader, and exuded joy at every turn. I asked Denard about the source of his eternal inner sunshine. He credited his parents, Thomas and Dorothea, and his entire family in Deerfield Beach, Florida.

"My parents, my brother, my whole family—we're never down," Robinson said. "That's just how we look at the world."

He loved attending Michigan basketball games and would frolic in the student section, shaking his head and dreadlocks from side to side and laughing out loud. He embraced everything Maize and Blue.

"I'm so glad to be a part of the tradition of this school," Robinson said. "Michigan tradition means you are part of a brotherhood, a family. We have our families back home, but we grow together and love each other here.

"Trust, respect, accountability, and commitment—those are the things we take to the field and try to embody. My proudest moment here has just been simply playing with my teammates."

And that 40–34 win over Ohio State—snapping a seven-game losing streak in the series—and 23–20 overtime win over Virginia Tech in the Sugar Bowl put Robinson and his teammates over the top with 11 wins in that comeback season of 2011.

Robinson had 337 yards total offense and accounted for five touchdowns against the Buckeyes. He was limited by the Hokies' relentless defense in New Orleans, but he did throw clutch 45- and 18-yard touchdown passes to Junior Hemingway, the game's MVP. And Brendan Gibbons booted three field goals, including the game-winner in overtime from 37 yards out.

"My freshman year, we didn't even go to a bowl game," Robinson said. "It meant so much to send those seniors out with those wins. We won a BCS bowl and beat Ohio! That was awesome."

Robinson was readying for the NFL draft and moving into a new position while also taking five classes to finish up his general studies degree with a sociology major in his final semester of school in 2013. But he still had time to meet with recruits coming through Ann Arbor.

"His message to the team and the recruits is so positive," Hoke said. "He tells them what the Michigan program is all about, and his impact on the program has been huge."

What is Robinson's message to recruits?

"When you first get here," Robinson said, "you are humbled down. They always get the cream of the crop at Michigan. Even if you are a five-star recruit, you have to work for what you get here. But it's all worth it. I tell them to embody the tradition, let it be fun, and enjoy your time here.

"But it all comes back to the coach. Brady sells himself by being honest and straight-forward. He's so genuine, a real person. He's straight with you and makes this a family. It's what made me love him right away.

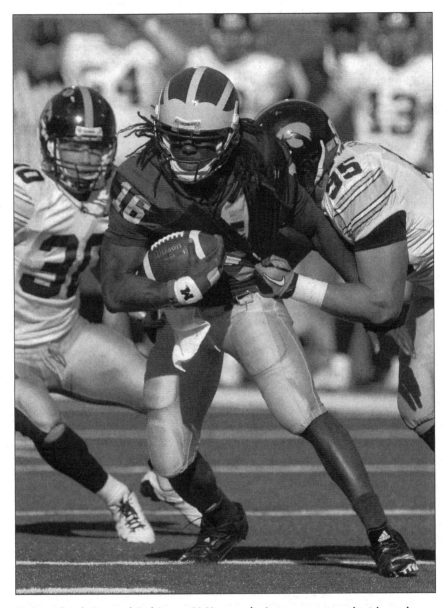

Quarterback Denard Robinson (16) runs during a game against Iowa in Ann Arbor, Michigan, on October 16, 2010. (AP Photo/Carlos Osorio)

He brings energy every day and is excited to be there with us. This is his dream job, the last job he wants to have.

"He tests us like a father, and I felt like his son. He told us when he came, 'Nobody has a position. You've got to work for it.' And that's what I wanted—the challenge is what I like."

DENARD IN THE NFL

When I spoke with San Francisco 49ers coach Jim Harbaugh about his years with the Wolverines, the former Michigan All-American quarterback was watching videotape of Denard Robinson.

"I see Denard on offense as a slot receiver and punt returner," Harbaugh said. "He definitely has the feet and speed for punt returns, and he is developing his route running. And quarterback-driven runs are more prevalent in the NFL now. He fits for sure."

CHAPTER 29

Greg Mattison:
Repairing a Defense and a Granddaughter's Heart

Plugging the holes in the Michigan defense was a daunting task.

The Wolverines, in Rich Rodriguez's third and final year as head coach, became an embarrassment. Michigan was outscored 137–49 in his final three games in 2010, including losses to Wisconsin, Ohio State, and Mississippi State in the Gator Bowl.

The Wolverines allowed 458 points that year—an average of five touchdowns per game. Michigan had not allowed even 300 points in a season until Rodriguez arrived and gave up at least 330 points per season during his brief stay as head coach.

Hoke hiring Baltimore Ravens defensive coordinator Greg Mattison to revive that defense was as important as Michigan athletic director Dave Brandon hiring Hoke. In the very next season, with essentially the same players, Mattison cut the points allowed in half. That was a phenomenal accomplishment. Michigan allowed only 226 points—an average of two touchdowns and one field goal per game.

"The players are the ones who did that, improved the defense," Mattison said. "They bought in and that group of seniors—led by Mike Martin and Ryan Van Bergen—made it happen. To not play great defense at Michigan was unheard of.

"We got the players to run to the football. We told them, 'You've got to play harder!' And they did. We had tremendous schemes, and they stayed with them."

Mattison also credited Wolverines offensive coordinator Al Borges and quarterback Denard Robinson. "Denard put points on the scoreboard, and Al did a good job of running the ball at times to keep the clock running and keep the defense off the field for a bit," Mattison said. "We're all in this together."

Michigan's offense clicked under Rodriguez with Robinson coming into his own in 2010 and the team amassing 426 points. But with Borges calling the plays for Robinson in a different offense, the Wolverines scored 433 points in 2011.

Linebacker Kenny Demens led the team with 94 tackles. Tackle-end Van Bergen was tops with 5½ sacks and 12½ tackles for lost yardage, and free safety Thomas Gordon either forced or recovered six total fumbles. Strong safety Jordan Kovacs made plays all over the field, and tackle Martin demanded double-teaming and still wreaked havoc. Cornerback J.T. Floyd broke up eight passes and intercepted two. Freshmen outside linebacker Jake Ryan and cornerback Blake Countess began showing their great promise, while end Craig Roh also stepped up to make impact plays.

"It was so neat to see the looks on their faces when they understood what it takes to be a Michigan football player and just where the bar is," Mattison said. "In this place, that's what we're made of. The bar is high."

Mattison is a grandfather, but he brings the enthusiasm of a high-motor player and exudes total confidence. He won the confidence of NFL stars such as Ray Lewis and Terrell Suggs while coaching the Ravens. Nobody has to convince the players he coaches or recruits that Mattison can make them everything they dream of being. He has total credibility and demands total dedication.

The Ravens won the Super Bowl two seasons after he left, and it was surprising that Mattison would leave a high-caliber NFL team like that to return to college. After all, he'd won a BCS national championship in 2006 as the co-defensive coordinator for Urban Meyer at the University of Florida. What did he have left to prove as a college defensive coordinator?

"If it had been to go with Brady and not at Michigan," Mattison said, "I would not have done it. If it had been to go back to Michigan but not with Brady, I wouldn't have done it.

"The Ravens was a tremendous job. I hadn't ever thought of being a pro coach, but I went for John Harbaugh. But I didn't get into coaching to just call defenses and put in a game plan. And what can I tell Ray Lewis and Terrell Suggs, really?"

Mattison, plain and simple, is a college coach. He wants to impact the lives of young men on and off the field.

"There are four reasons why I came back to Michigan," Mattison said. "First, I loved to hear a kid who developed come in as a senior and ask me who his agent should be. Second, I missed helping players earn their college degrees."

Mattison then turned and pointed to the shelf along the window sill of his Schembechler Hall office and the photos of the two-year-old granddaughters he adores along with his wife, Ann. He first pointed to Hadley, the daughter of his son, Bryan, who starred at Iowa and now plays defensive end for the Kansas City Chiefs. Then he pointed to the grinning Mattie Roberts, daughter of his daughter, Lisa, who was a three-time All-Big East first baseman for the Notre Dame softball team.

"Lisa named her Mattie," Greg said, "which is my nickname. She was born with a hole in her heart. Lisa called me when Brady got the job and said, 'Are you coming with Brady? I know you two are close.' Then she said, 'We moved with you on every job you ever took, Dad. I want you to come back.'" Lisa owns a shop, Rock Paper Scissors, about one mile from Michigan Stadium on Main Street.

Mattison's children grew up in the same neighborhood with mine, playing pickup football and basketball games together and forming friendships.

"You're a grandfather, too," Greg said to me. "You know about family and its importance. And then Dave Brandon tells me the greatest heart surgeon for the type of surgery Mattie needs is at the University of Michigan, and he will do the operation. After the surgery, he tells me, 'She will play softball just like your daughter. She's going to be fine.'"

Grandpa beamed, glancing back at Mattie's framed photo.

"It was just the right decision to come back—everything lined up," Mattison said. "But there was one more reason. Fourth, there was Brady. He's a very tough-minded coach, and he's a coach who stays true to his beliefs, demands, and course. Kids will jump on board for him. And being back together, it was all about once again establishing Michigan as we remembered it and making sure our guys become Michigan Men."

Mattison lined it up and saw all pros and no cons.

"He has loved Michigan since working there earlier in his career," Ravens coach John Harbaugh said in a statement. "Greg is one of the good people you are fortunate to meet in your life. We are disappointed that he will not be coaching our defense, but we know that he is following a true love by returning to the Wolverines."

Hoke and Mattison coached on one of the most impressive staffs ever assembled in the Mid-American Conference. Jack Harbaugh, the father of Wolverines All-American quarterback Jim Harbaugh, had both of them on his staff from 1984–86, and Jack also had his oldest son, John, coaching running backs and outside linebackers. John won the "Har-Bowl" Super Bowl in 2013 against Jim's San Francisco 49ers.

Current Michigan special teams coach Dan Ferrigno was the WMU offensive coordinator, Mattison was the defensive coordinator beginning in 1982, and Hoke coached the defensive line starting in 1984. It was Mattison who noticed Hoke while he was on the staff at Grand Valley State and was impressed with the way he presented himself while recruiting high school players. Mattison suggested Hoke to Jack Harbaugh, and the rest is history.

And yet with all that coaching firepower, they were all fired after going 3–8 in 1986.

"We were so close to putting it together there," Mattison said, "and

Head coach Brady Hoke (left) and defensive coordinator Greg Mattison watch during the fourth quarter of a game against Nebraska in Ann Arbor, Michigan, on Saturday, November 19, 2011. (AP Photo/Carlos Osorio)

they won it all when we left." Western Michigan went 9–3 and won the Mid-American Conference championship two years later in 1988.

Hoke moved on to coach at Toledo and Oregon State before Gary Moeller hired him at Michigan in February 1995. Mattison rebounded from Western Michigan to coach the defensive lines at Navy and Texas A&M before Moeller hired him in 1992 to coach his defensive line.

"I was the GA [graduate assistant] for Bob Blackman at Illinois in 1976 for the fall semester," Mattison said. "When Mo came in as the new coach at Illinois, he kept me. Lloyd Carr was on his new staff. I just loved Mo and Lloyd. It was a tremendous experience for me. Gary Moeller and Lloyd Carr are way, way up there on the list of college football coaches.

"Mo was something special. I just remember thinking, *Please don't let me let this guy down.*"

Both Hoke and Mattison learned much about becoming leaders that players and coaches naturally follow from Moeller and then Carr. And that is why they knew exactly how to bring Michigan back to being Michigan.

Mattison was motivated by the greatness around him at Schembechler Hall, and that goes for the times when the building's namesake dropped by.

"I was making copies one time and Bo walked in behind me," said Mattison, who re-enacted that moment, acting nervously and turning his head from side to side while gathering copies from an imaginary machine.

"I'm thinking, *This is Bo Schembechler here*. I turned around and Bo says, 'Hey, you're doing a good job. Keep it up!' I'm thinking, *Oh my God, this is the absolute best coach*."

Mattison came back to uphold what Bo built for the players he coached, his close friend the head coach, and the little girl whose heart was repaired as surely as the Michigan defense.

CHAPTER 30

Brady Hoke:
Leading with Love

What caught my attention about Brady Hoke—even more than going 11–2 in his first season at Michigan—is what he does on Senior Day in Ann Arbor. Hoke goes down the long line of players at midfield and exchanges pleasantries with them and their families before hugging and planting a kiss on the cheek of each and every player.

He becomes as much a second father or an uncle to the Wolverines as he is their head coach, and that kind of relationship is something only a genuine, compassionate man can build with his players. Those qualities are what college athletics should be all about. That way, whether the team wins or loses, the players gain something bigger than football games. They get a friend and mentor for life—a man they can always go to with the good and bad things that are sure to come their way.

There are only two ways to lead—through fear or love. And Hoke has chosen the latter.

"That love I show is part of the fabric of who I am," Hoke said. "It's how I was raised in an honest, loving home. Sometimes being honest can hurt you. But we'll always support and help you. We truly get invested with our kids."

So there was Hoke, hugging and kissing Will Campbell, the 6'5", 315-lb. defensive tackle, before the Iowa game in 2012. Campbell's growth flashed through the coach's mind.

"I coached him daily and saw him develop a love for his teammates

Offensive lineman David Molk (50) shares a word with head coach Brady Hoke during a break in the fourth quarter of a game against Ohio State on Saturday, November 26, 2011, in Ann Arbor. Michigan won 40-34. (AP Photo/Tony Ding)

and develop his body," Hoke said. "He went from 350 to 315 pounds. There was some major work he put in, switching positions [between the offensive and defensive lines and even some fullback]. He showed great leadership and played great with great effort."

Hoke mentioned how special it was to interact not only with Campbell but with players you probably never heard of—like reserve receiver Steve Wilson and quarterback Jack Kennedy. And then there was Jordan Kovacs, a four-year starter who came to Ann Arbor without a scholarship and left with great respect, admiration, and 193 tackles.

"Kovacs had to walk on twice in this program," Hoke said. "How could you not love him?"

Hoke said he learned about love and honesty from his parents, John and Pat, while growing up south of Dayton in Kettering, Ohio. His father wasn't afraid to show love and kissed his sons on the cheek. Jon Hoke, his older brother, is the defensive backs coach of the Chicago Bears.

"My father, who died last year, was old school," Hoke said. "He was a teacher and a football and baseball coach. He showed me that honesty is just so essential with people, teammates, everybody. And I learned from Dad that there are different ways to motivate, and every person is motivated differently. But you have to have a consistency and clarity in your message."

We met at Schembechler Hall during spring practice in 2013, and we talked while seated on some comfortable leather chairs in a lounge that adjoins Hoke's office. He wore shorts and a T-shirt in the school colors, and he often leaned back with both hands behind his neck and smiled easily. Hoke wanted to know about the path I had taken since leaving the Michigan football beat during his first years as an assistant in Ann Arbor, and his interest was genuine.

So in a matter of minutes, I could see why Hoke is a premier recruiter. He relates to you quickly without it coming across as a sell job. He reminded me a lot of Gary Moeller, the head coach who hired him as an assistant at Michigan. Hoke is a meat-and-potatoes guy who exudes trust and passion.

"Brady's always been a great recruiter because he works so hard at it and the relationships," former Michigan offensive coordinator Mike DeBord said. "That has been his bloodline."

Every college football coach in the country tells parents that he will treat their son like his own son. Some do, and some don't. But Hoke leaves no doubt that he means it.

"I tell parents that with us, what you see is what you get," Hoke said.

And that parental leaning came through when I asked for his reaction to getting his dream job as the head coach at Michigan on January 11, 2011. "It was flattering and humbling," Hoke said. "But the first thing I said was, 'I've got a job to do. I've got 115 sons waiting for me.'"

How did a boy from Ohio who grew up during the height of Buckeyes coach Woody Hayes' rule in that state come to love the Wolverines? "I started rooting for Michigan when I was 10 because I wanted to be different," Hoke said. "My dad played at Miami of Ohio for Woody Hayes [and alongside Bo Schembechler], and all my friends rooted for Woody's team."

And he takes the rivalry to extremes. He refers to them as Ohio, dropping the State. "Brady always had a great love for Michigan," said DeBord, now the administrator for nine athletic teams at Michigan. "He had it when he came, left, and came back.

"Do you know he would only wear all black at Ball State and San Diego State [where he served as head coach before coming to Michigan], which both had red in their school colors. He didn't wear red because of Ohio State. That was a sign of his love for Michigan. When you have a guy who absolutely loves the school he is working for, you have a special fit."

I mentioned this aversion to red to Hoke.

"No," he said, sticking his tongue in his cheek, "I don't own any red clothing."

Hoke said his love for the school intensified while working Michigan's summer football camps when he was an assistant at Grand Valley State and Schembechler was still the head coach. And in 1995, Moeller hired Hoke as an assistant coach.

"I had an 11½-hour interview here," Hoke said, "and 4½ hours of it was with Gary Moeller. We talked about life, about life's lessons. We talked about football technique and football skills. I loved it, and at the end, I said, 'I want this job.' Gary looked at me and said, 'You know, some people think we are arrogant.'"

Hoke leaned back and extended both hands, saying, "I didn't know if it was a statement or a question. But Gary just picked it up from there and said, 'They should, and they are right. We're Michigan.'"

Hoke left Ann Arbor not knowing if he got the job, but in less than one week Moeller called to say it was his. Hoke coached players on the defensive front through the 2002 season and was part of three Big Ten champions and one national champion. He coached three All-Americans in Will Carr (1996), Glen Steele (1997), and Rob Renes (1999).

But Hoke wanted to be a head coach, and the perfect opportunity arose at his alma mater, Ball State. It was his ability to love that also impressed the folks in Muncie, Indiana.

"Brady Hoke loves hard," FOXSports.com columnist Jason Whitlock wrote in 2011. "He loves his family, his players, his assistant coaches, Ball State football, and Michigan football."

Whitlock, who played at Ball State one decade after Hoke, helped the school's athletic director at the time, Bubba Cunningham, identify Hoke as the top candidate for the head coach opening in 2003. Hoke was chosen over Kansas State assistant Brett Bielema, who would go on to win Big Ten titles at Wisconsin before becoming the Arkansas coach in 2013. Hoke started slow at Ball State but finished with a school record for victories at 12–1 in 2008.

"Eight years ago," Whitlock wrote in 2011, "Brady and I became family. I love the dude. I love his wife, his daughter, his parents, his brother, his nephew, his niece, and the way he looks and sounds like

Fred Flintstone."

And he's definitely a bedrock of a football coach. Hoke built a sound foundation at Ball State and San Diego State, where he coached for two seasons before getting the Michigan job. The Aztecs were 9–4 and won a bowl game in his final season.

Hoke has an ability to instantly win trust, supply excellent coaching, and rally a team.

"He's always had a great relationship with his players," DeBord said. "Guys like Glen Steele played harder for him than other coaches. The guy just has everything in perspective. He was just as happy as the defensive line coach as he was as the head coach. He's not caught up in titles."

In fact, Hoke is the Michigan inside linebackers coach. He's coached a position group in addition to being the head coach every year since his first one as the head coach at Ball State. Hoke is not a tower-viewing coach; he's hands-on.

"It keeps me connected," Hoke said. "It keeps me close to the players." He also won't wear anything other than a short-sleeve coaching polo shirt on the sidelines no matter how cold it might be. But there's much more to him than unabashed love and plenty of quirks.

Wolverines defensive coordinator Greg Mattison, who recommended Hoke for his first Division I coaching job at Western Michigan in 1984, said his success is rooted in passion and selflessness. "Kids love Brady because they know he's real," Mattison said. "Brady has nothing at all to do with the word I."

Steve Hutchinson, an All-American offensive guard in 2000 who moved from defensive tackle after redshirting in 1996, is typical of the players who have bonded with Hoke. "Brady was a father figure for me and many of the guys that played during my time at Michigan," Hutchinson, a seven-time Pro Bowl selection with the Seattle Seahawks and Minnesota Vikings, said in a comment featured in the team's 2012 media guide. "He always looked out for his players and taught us to act with character. Brady is one of the reasons why I've had the success that

I've had in my career.

"Learning how to do things the right way was a direct result of being around Brady.... I know that he will do extremely well and represent this university with class and integrity."

Hoke gets players on board quickly. "That first-year turnaround was unbelievable," DeBord said. "But his success here did not and never will surprise me."

Hoke's four-win improvement on the 2010 season's 7–6 record tied the legendary Fielding H. Yost's school record. Yost went 11–0 with his first season in 1901, coming off a 7–2–1 campaign by head coach Langdon "Biff" Lea.

Moeller lost his job before ever coaching a game with Hoke on his staff, but Hoke served under Lloyd Carr as defensive ends, defensive line, and associate head coach for eight seasons.

"You know, talk about a coach who loved his players," Hoke said. "Lloyd was very emotional and loved his players and his team. They loved him, and still love him."

Moeller's and Bo's players also had a lasting love with their coach. That's a common thread between the school's great coaches of the last half century. Only none of them gave their players a peck on the cheek on Senior Day, though. That's Hoke's special touch.

"I'm proud of what we've done here in two seasons," Hoke said. "But we've got a long way to go. We have a great staff. Our kids understand what a Michigan degree is all about, and have a passion to represent 133 years of Michigan football tradition.

"But the 8–5 last year—that isn't good enough at Michigan. We have to do better than that."

The season didn't end with the kind of record desired—far from it. But it did have a fitting ending in the Big House with a win over Iowa and that emotional good-bye to the seniors.

On Senior Day, Hoke unveiled charismatic quarterback Denard Robinson as a running back after giving him his Senior Day salute and affection. "Denard had to change offenses and embraced it," Hoke said. "I looked at him on Senior Day and said, 'I'm proud of you.' He said, 'I love you,' and I kissed him on the cheek.

"Some of the guys are shocked when I kiss them, but most of them say, 'I love you, too.'"

Robinson was touched. "I appreciate that love from him because Brady Hoke is a genuine man," Robinson told me. "I saw him doing that, kissing each of us as he came down the line, and I thought, *We're just kids and we're his sons.*

"That's a pretty special feeling."

A Special Valentine's Day

Brady and Laura Hoke were childhood sweethearts in Kettering, Ohio.

"We dated since the seventh grade," Brady said.

When Michigan athletic director Dave Brandon called to tell him the job as head coach was his in 2011, Brady let it ring until Laura got home. He wanted her there to hear the good news with him.

When she was carrying their first and only child on Valentine's Day in 1985, Brady was an assistant coach at Western Michigan and stuck in a blizzard in Fort Wayne, Indiana. Schools were closed and he was having trouble collecting national letters of intent, but the mother of one recruit told him she had an important message from Western Michigan's head coach, Jack Harbaugh.

"I looked down at the number she handed me but I did not recognize it as Jack's," Hoke said. "I called and Jack was at the hospital. He said, 'You have a baby girl. Get back up here to Kalamazoo, but be careful and take your time.'

"Kelly was premature and weighed only 1 pound and 8 ounces. She was in an incubator when I got there, and Jack Harbaugh was keeping my whole family together. He had been calling the Indiana State Police to try to find me. We didn't have cellphones back then.

"He still calls my daughter every year on Valentine's Day to wish her happy birthday. Jack and Jackie Harbaugh are unbelievable people, a great couple. It was one of the busiest days of the year, but he left his job to be there for me. That's Jack."

ACKNOWLEDGMENTS

I would like to thank Lloyd Carr, Gary Moeller, Brady Hoke, Greg Mattison, Mike DeBord, Joe Roberson, Jim Harbaugh, Tyrone Wheatley, Denard Robinson, Mark Messner, Tom Hemingway, Jim Brandstatter, Frank Beckmann, and Jim Schneider for being interviewed for this book. And I would like to credit Bruce Madej, Dave Ablauf, Justin Dickens, Tara Preston, and Greg Kinney of the University of Michigan for helping connect me to sources and archived articles. Zingerman's Deli in Ann Arbor, where Carr and I met for lunches and cups of tea and coffee, supplied a comfortable setting for conversation and should be recognized for its hospitality.

I'd also like to express gratitude to the editors who worked with me while covering the Wolverines for the *Ann Arbor News*, *Booth Newspapers*, and the *Detroit Free Press*: the late Wayne DeNeff, Brian Malone, Dave Robinson, Owen Davis, and Gene Myers. And a special mention to several writing friends who encouraged me while I was undertaking this labor of love: Tom Gage, Mitch Albom, Mike Happy, Bob "Bubba" Black, John Lowe, Mike Heidner, Jayson Stark, Charles Hollis, Tom Maloney, Jason Beck, Bayard Steele, and Penny Carnathan.

Four very close friends have long encouraged me to write a book, and for that spark I would like to thank my cousin, Stan Kornacki, plus Bill Branks, Steve McConihay, and Hjalma Johnson.

Teachers, who have the most important jobs in the world, also contributed to my love of writing at an early age. Dennis Hamilton, who taught creative writing at Trenton (Michigan) High, and Eastern Michigan University journalism instructors Helen "Taffy" Larcom and Bernie Decker must be acknowledged for getting me on the right track.

Go Blue!

And I also would like to express a heartfelt thanks to all those who have read my stories at the *Monroe Evening News*, the *Ann Arbor News*, *Detroit Free Press*, *Orlando Sentinel*, *Oakland Press*, *Tampa Tribune*, *Booth Newspapers*, MLive.com, and now at FOXSportsDetroit.com. Your encouragement and readership have allowed me to tell stories for a living. And for that, I am forever grateful.

NOTES

CHAPTER 1

Information was used from the author's by-lined story in the November 23, 1989, *Detroit Free Press*.

CHAPTER 2

Information was used from the author's by-lined stories in the September 5, 1985, *Ann Arbor News*, December 8, 1986, *Ann Arbor News*, December 16, 1989, *Detroit Free Press*, and November 18, 2006, *Tampa Tribune*.

CHAPTER 3

Bo Schembechler Behind Closed Doors: Information in this section came from the Washington Redskins' website.

Information in this chapter came from the author's by-lined stories in the *Ann Arbor News*, September 5, 1985, January 2, 1986, and December 8, 1986, and the *Tampa Tribune*, November 18, 2006.

CHAPTER 5

Information was used from the author's by-lined stories in the *Ann Arbor News*, November 23, 1986, and October 30, 1985.

CHAPTER 6

Information was used from the author's by-lined story in the September 25, 1985, *Ann Arbor News*.

CHAPTER 7

Information was used from the author's by-lined stories in the *Ann Arbor News*, November 10, 1985, and November 24, 1985.

CHAPTER 8
Information used from the author's story in the *Ann Arbor News*, August 14, 1988.

CHAPTER 10
Information was used from the author's by-lined story in the December 13, 1991, *Detroit Free Press*.

CHAPTER 11
Information was used from the author's by-lined story in the *Detroit Free Press* on December 13, 1991.

CHAPTER 14
Hurricane Andrew Took Everything but Their Lives, Dogs, and Gator Bowl MVP Trophy: Information for this section was used from the author's by-lined stories in the *Detroit Free Press* on December 30, 1991, November 4, 1992, and April 26, 1993.

CHAPTER 15
Information from the author's *Detroit Free Press* stories from January 2, 1993, August 26, 1992, and January 1, 1989.

CHAPTER 17
Information used from the author's by-lined story in the *Detroit Free Press*, September 21, 1994.

CHAPTER 20
Information used from the author's by-lined *Detroit Free Press* story from November 22, 1995.

CHAPTER 27
Information was used from the author's by-lined *Detroit Free Press* story on September 26, 1994.

SOURCES

BOOKS

Brandstatter, Jim. *Tales from Michigan Stadium, vol. 1 and 2.* Champaign, IL: Sports Publishing LLC, 2002.

Hemmingway, Tom. *Life Among the Wolverines.* Diamond Communications, 1985.

Kipling, Rudyard. *The Jungle Book.* London: Macmillan Publishers, 1894.

Krakauer, Jon. *Into Thin Air.* New York: Villard Books, 1997.

MAGAZINES

The Sporting News
Sports Illustrated

NEWSPAPERS

Baltimore Sun
Detroit Free Press
Ann Arbor News
Detroit News
Augusta (Ga.) *Chronicle*
San Francisco Examiner
Tampa Tribune

WEBSITES

www.espn.com
www.mgoblue.com
www.redskins.com
www.ufer.org
www.nfl.com
Wikipedia

OTHER

University of Michigan Sports Information department and its publications.

INDEX

Index

ABOUT THE AUTHOR

Steve Kornacki covered the University of Michigan football beat at *The Ann Arbor News* and *Detroit Free Press*, telling gripping stories and breaking news on the Wolverines over two decades. He wrote about Heisman Trophy winners Desmond Howard and Charles Woodson, and the 1997 national champion-ship team. Kornacki grew up in Trenton, Michigan, and first met Michigan football coach Lloyd Carr while attending Eastern Michigan University and writing as the sports editor of the *Eastern Echo*. He also wrote and or edited at the *Tampa Tribune* and *Orlando Sentinel*, serves as a *Sports Illustrated* correspondent, and currently is chronicling the exploits of the Detroit Tigers and Michigan State for FOXSportsDetroit.com